FOLLOW
THIS
PATH

Other Books from
The Gallup Organization

First, Break All the Rules:
What the World's Greatest Managers Do Differently
by Marcus Buckingham and Curt Coffman

Now, Discover Your Strengths
by Marcus Buckingham and Donald O. Clifton, Ph.D.

FOLLOW THIS PATH

HOW THE WORLD'S GREATEST ORGANIZATIONS DRIVE GROWTH BY UNLEASHING HUMAN POTENTIAL

CURT COFFMAN and GABRIEL GONZALEZ-MOLINA, Ph.D.

WARNER
BUSINESS
BOOKS™

Published by Warner Books

An AOL Time Warner Company

WARNER BOOKS EDITION

Copyright © 2002 by The Gallup Organization
All rights reserved.

 Warner Business Books are published by Warner Books, Inc., 1271 Avenue of the Americas, New York, NY 10020

Visit our Web site at www.twbookmark.com.

 An AOL Time Warner Company

Printed in the United States of America
First International Trade Printing: October 2002
10 9 8 7 6 5 4 3 2 1

ISBN 0-446-69035-X

Book design by Giorgetta Bell McRee
Cover design by Brigid Pearson
Cover photo by Herman Estevez

For my beautiful and very talented wife, Tammy,
whose strength, challenge, and love
have always kept my purpose clear.
—Curt W. Coffman

For the emotional memory of Ignacio and Josefina,
my parents.
For Belinda, Gabriel, and Jose Ignacio,
the emotional markers of my lifetime.
—Gabriel Gonzalez-Molina

CONTENTS

Contents

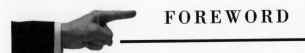

FOREWORD

I am haunted by a two-inch graph that appeared recently in *The Economist*. Although the graph is small and very simple, it could be the most important business story this executive has ever seen. I cannot understand why it was not on the front page of every newspaper in America.

Maybe everyone knows why except me. Here is the graph.

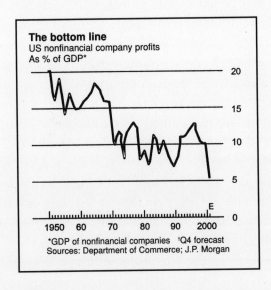

The bottom line
US nonfinancial company profits
As % of GDP*

*GDP of nonfinancial companies †Q4 forecast
Sources: Department of Commerce; J.P. Morgan

The Economist, December 8, 2001, p. 65.

You and I do not need to send this graph to our research departments for translation. It tracks the "percent" of profit of all nonfinancial companies in the United States over the last fifty years. One thing you could do is apply a little math to determine when American free enterprise will go broke.

What you see is a relentless fifty-year force gradually squashing the profit out of American companies. It is a monster stalking each and every one of us. Now, all of us have our time in the sun, when our product is unique, we have a strong market share, and we enjoy almost no clear competition. This situation might be driven by anything from great innovation to simply being the first to open pizza parlors in our neck of the woods. Or it might be the result of government regulations that suddenly enable us to achieve decent margins.

For example, at one point in history Dr. Gallup offered the only poll in the country. He made terrific margins as virtually the only game in town. Now there are roughly five-thousand organizations offering the same methodologies. The same thing has happened in lots of other industries. I remember when the telephone bills at Gallup were 30 cents per minute; AT&T charged us $3 to conduct a ten-minute interview. We now pay about 3 cents a minute to MCI. So a ten-minute interview costs us 30 cents compared to $3.

The frightening question is: Are we great customer managers or have we just talked a good game at company conferences, and at the end of the day become merely the world's biggest price slashers? The story of "the graph" is that you make your discoveries, build your new inventions, make great margins, and then ride the razor blade down to zero.

Again, the conclusions and implications from this graph tell a thousand stories—all of them haunting.

Let's go back to the telephone industry. Was this industry driven by twenty years of magnificent marketing and leadership by AT&T and MCI, and eventually Sprint, or was it driven simply by MCI slashing the once great margins of Ma

Bell? Did WorldCom take over because its chief could some-how endure the razor-blade ride longer, and therefore keep slashing prices? Were the telephone wars just twenty years of controlled price slashing? Could the same be said of auto-mobiles, computers, retailing, and on and on?

Recently, we have all developed great expertise as "cost cut-ters." We were terrible at this twenty-five years ago, but we lis-tened closely to Dr. Edwards Deming and Dr. Joseph Juran, and they showed us how to greatly lower production costs—brilliantly—by "reducing variation." We supported this move-ment because it meant we could cut prices more. It slowed our ride down the razor blade.

"Reengineering." We all did this and it also worked. In fact, we saved a bunch of money at Gallup by applying the theories of both of these significant corporate leadership movements.

We have been quick to learn how to cut prices, but we have learned virtually nothing about how to grow margins. This ignorance leads to a desperation that accompanies lead-ership as it rides the razor blade. In fact, while penciling these thoughts early in 2002, this worried executive won-dered if this sense of desperation has produced the current epidemic of financial reporting chicanery. At some point we may all experience ethical cracks when the pressure is too much to bear. We are led to this desperate state by the fear of losing money—not because we are natural-born thieves. Sick companies crack under the pressure of riding the razor blade. Apparently, it is much easier to hoodwink sharehold-ers than customers.

So here's the problem: We can't maintain our margins from normal operations when we are faced with extreme competition. What causes the problem? A customer relation-ship based solely on price. When all you have that differen-tiates you is your price, you are a commodity.

What is the solution? You have to have a relationship with

customers that to some degree overrides price. If not, you will slowly, then suddenly, go broke.

Yes, you should use all the latest cost-cutting techniques and reengineering-type processes to improve efficiencies as much as possible. But these processes do not provide the long-term solution to maintaining your margins.

Again, the ultimate solution to reversing the current leadership trends of margin slashing, accounting trickery, and shareholder hoodwinking is to run an organization that can maintain and expand its customer base without slashing prices and without reducing its fiscal integrity.

The success of your organization doesn't depend on your understanding of economics, or organizational development, or marketing. It depends, quite simply, on your understanding of psychology: how each individual employee connects with *your company;* how each individual employee connects with *your customers.*

Ask yourself: Why do employees stay with one company when others are willing to pay them more? Why do some employees innately know how to deal with customer complaints, without alienating those customers? Why do some customers drive three miles out of the way to come to your store when your competitor is right across the street from them? If you don't know the answers to these questions, you cannot maintain your margins.

Put in another way, you must harness the power of human nature or you can never get down from the razor-blade ride.

The extraordinary American economy of the last fifty years has been based on remarkable innovation and entrepreneurship. There is no substitute for these. However, in the new world of extreme competition, we are all going down the wrong path—the one toward continuous margin erosion—unless we discover a new way to manage human nature.

This book does exactly that. It outlines the steps that leaders must take to build strong, sustainable, high-integrity organizations. By cracking the human nature code, it offers an entirely new and different "Path" for your organization to follow. Read the book as quickly as you can, follow this Path, and rejoin your organization as a transformed leader.

—James K. Clifton
Chairman and Chief Executive Officer
The Gallup Organization
January 15, 2002

FOLLOW THIS PATH

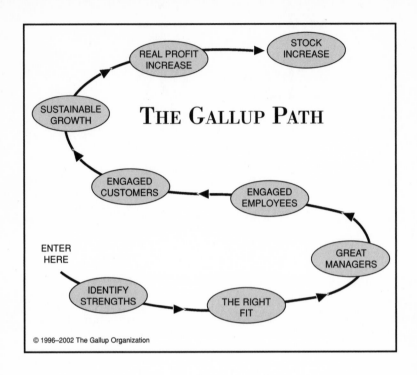

THE GALLUP PATH

REAL PROFIT INCREASE

STOCK INCREASE

SUSTAINABLE GROWTH

ENGAGED CUSTOMERS

ENGAGED EMPLOYEES

GREAT MANAGERS

ENTER HERE

IDENTIFY STRENGTHS

THE RIGHT FIT

The Path to Take

Great organizations achieve sustainable growth and profits because they do what other organizations don't: They maximize the innate, individual talents of their employees to connect with customers. They know that tapping the resources of humans is the only remaining area where significant improvements can—and do—lead to an unlimited source of competitive advantages.

Startling? Yes.

Against the accepted way of doing business? Absolutely.

Successful? You bet.

Will this change the way you view employees and customers alike? It should—*if* you want to profit and grow along with the great organizations and compete with them.

Now Is the Time for Change

In case you haven't noticed, there's a whole new world of employees and customers out there. Where employees are concerned, the modern workplace is not filled with a generation of workers who received identical marching orders: Get an education so that you'll be hired for a steady job at a decent salary. Work as hard as you possibly can, because a job is a privilege on which you can base your future and secure the welfare of your family. The perceived value of hard work, discipline, and responsibility should never waver. Your "loyalty" will be taken for granted.

Recalled a man who repaired underground cables:

> I worked for a major utility for thirty years. I remember being told how lucky I was to be hired. Whenever I received a raise, I felt obliged to tell my boss how grateful I felt. I was, too. But it would have been nice to hear how grateful they were to me [for] working, winter and summer, under all kinds of tough conditions. I guess they felt they didn't have to—so they didn't.

Of course they didn't, because the employer held unyielding power: "I, as an employer, do not need you as much as you need me. I can fire you whenever I please, take away your job security, and ruin your financial health. Imagine what I can do to you—and your family."

This was the not-so-subtle message that many employees received along with their first paycheck. So the employees toed the line. Within the framework of an oversupply of labor and scarce jobs, they tended to stay put for the long haul and "learn the rules," adjusting their behavior and productivity along the way. Greater productivity meant working harder to get more done. Even in times of prosperity, workers never forgot that the organization was king. If their particular talents were best suited to another job, very often they kept that secret to themselves.

And where customers were concerned, the situation wasn't much better. Monopolies ruled. Providing a product or service to the marketplace meant ownership of an industry. Customers couldn't choose, because they were forced to buy products or services from a single supplier. With no other options available, loyalty was ensured. With that assurance, executives and senior managers focused very little of their attention on satisfying the needs of their customers.

A woman who purchased all of her appliances from the one local store for over twenty years told us:

> I always thought of myself as a "loyal" customer. Service wasn't great, but when a mall was built and a big appliance store with lots of different brands opened, I felt that I should remain a customer of my local store. But I found that the bigger store had friendlier employees who made me feel like I was important and what I bought mattered. Sure, the lower prices counted, but I felt so much more appreciated at the new store. Why should I feel like I should accept subpar service if I don't have to?

A New Model

Today the world of work has totally changed. Nowadays people skip from job to job and from company to company. Working as hard as possible may still be an ideal held by some, but too often they burn out quickly and lose their effectiveness. Just about everyone sitting at a computer has access to the same technology. Privacy, especially relating to company secrets, is harder to maintain, as is its partner, security.

Industry is no longer a one-size-fits-all proposition. Diversification is not a luxury but often a hard necessity. Calculating productivity, growth, earnings, market capitalization, or stockholder value requires complex formulas and hourly updates from the industrial front. Television networks have expanded their business coverage because the world's economy is a tanker riding choppy waves. At any time that ship, as big and powerful as it is, can spring a leak or run aground.

Customers who could once be counted on now enjoy

choices—a whole lot of them. Monopolies are relics. Industries once regulated—telecommunications, auto manufacturing, and health care, to name just three—are now deregulated. And where competition is concerned, the playing field, with its rules, is global. The gradual but steady elimination of cultural and international boundaries has opened up worldwide marketplaces. Now businesses must compete with their counterparts from other countries for the same customers. This requires broader income to fund the development of more useful products and services. At the same time organizations must maintain their image through brands and positioning.

And that creates a new dilemma. In the past twenty years almost every possible source of competitive advantage has been maxed out. Where can value be found when price becomes less and less of a factor, and customers are tired of hearing that every product or service is the "best"? They know better. Where both employee and customer incentives are concerned, organizations are running on empty.

But more than ever, a reliable customer base, the core element of every industry, must be maintained. At the same time productive employees must be kept from leaving.

But how? What strategy could possibly do this? The great organizations have discovered what it is—and how to use it.

An Emotion-Driven Economy

Great organizations know how to chart a course through the worldwide competitive maze to keep their customer relationships not only intact but also thriving. They do this by connecting to their customers on an emotional level. When that happens, customers return because of *the way they feel*. The response has been so phenomenal that these organizations don't refer to their return patrons as loyal. They speak of them as being *emotionally engaged customers*.

Simultaneously, great organizations create an environment

in which their best performers can do what they excel at, over and over again. These men and women are so tuned in to what they are doing, and so effective at responding to the needs of customers, that profits and growth flourish, as do the employees. These men and women are referred to, with gratitude, as being *emotionally engaged employees.*

When engaged employees utilize their natural talents, they provide an instant, and constant, competitive edge. They build a new value: emotionally driven connections between employees and customers.

Great organizations do not treat employees and customers as if they are mini computers whose every action, based on very complex mental processes, can be calculated in advance. Nor do they view customers as "economic agents" who are supposed to always make decisions based on price and quantity.

On the contrary, great organizations have turned from the "hard" view of people responding like machines to the "soft" side of human nature, the part that is guided by emotions. Engaging both employees and customers emotionally is the approach that steers organizations, through their managers, toward greatness. Great organizations take advantage of the fact that the economy of emotional engagement is much bigger than the economy of reason.

The Data Are Here

How do we know that an emotion-driven economy leads to continued success? For more than fifty years The Gallup Organization has asked customers and employees alike a huge variety of questions about jobs, the workplace, and decisions related to purchases and consumption. We queried every major type of industry, conducting research on a global scale.

When we at Gallup began our immense and far-reaching study, we aimed to uncover the circumstances that separated the strongest, most vibrant, productive, and profitable workplaces from the not-so-dynamic ones. At the same time we wanted to discover the conditions that attracted—and kept—the finest, most profitable customers. These were the people whose human potential had been given a free rein, and they put it to extremely good use. We wanted to estimate the economic implications of the variation between the great workplaces and the rest. And what great organizations do to create more of the best.

Finding the information we sought within the swirling patterns of data wasn't simple, because every organization defined successful outcomes in its own way. For some of the best workplaces, results meant the number of customer problems solved, whereas for others they reflected recovery time of patients, increased sales volume, number of defects per million parts produced, or number of days lost to illness. Turnover and the productivity of individuals were factored into the equation.

Enormous amounts of data were collected to conduct our inquiry. Ten million customers and over two hundred thousand managers were surveyed. More than three million employees were interviewed from 1995 through 2001. Additionally, more than two million talent-fit/role-success reviews were tallied. More than 300,000 business units, in hundreds of organizations worldwide, took part in the study. Not surprisingly, the total volume of data surpassed that of any other study on the subject of specific employee performance and building of customer loyalty.

All major industries, from fast-food chains to physicians' groups, were represented. A wide variety of job types was included, as were all kinds of customers. Industry and organizations of all sizes were integrated. To give this some sense of scale, consider that each major industry represented contributed at least one hundred thousand cases, while the business units were usually comprised of just thirteen employees. Employees from different types of organizations were measured in terms of their talent, engagement, and outcomes.

Similarly, customer data included purchase information: Volume, dollar amounts spent, repurchase intentions and behavior, brand ratings, product evaluations, opinions, and other complementary patterns of attitudes and behavior were all covered in detail.

For the customer data alone each person questioned was interviewed for an average of fifteen minutes, which led to an incredible 150 million minutes of individual responses. Think of it this way: If each response was equal to one square inch of a customer's report, the total data represented the equivalent of covering an entire football field twenty-four times.

Business units were evaluated in terms of their productivity, volume (revenue, sales, and quotas), safety, turnover, and profits per unit. Other related information, such as size of the location, was gathered as well.

This in-depth study also crossed gender, race, and ethnicity boundaries as it assembled data on various types of occupations, nationalities, age groups, levels of education and discretionary income, and spending habits.

To untie this complicated knot of information we used meta-analysis. (A detailed description of the types of statistical techniques used appears in appendix B.) This statistical technique helped us untangle and separate the multiple strands of data. Using it allowed us to zero in on the real links between employee attitudes and opinions and business unit performance. Additionally, we were able to document how certain conditions (which we will disclose later on) affect business outcomes. We were also able to detect the unmistakable symptoms of a workplace on the verge of breakdown due to ingrained negative business practices. And we developed a surefire ability to identify those core sources of strength that every great team inherently possesses. Most important, we recognized how unbreakable bonds between employees and customers can be forged.

Then this mother lode of data was examined and dissected. When we were done, we saw the way that great organizations mine and harness the incredible natural resources of their employees. The steps were the same, over and over again. They formed an explicit way in which *every* great organization utilizes employees and keeps customers—regardless of its size, industry, or country of origin. We discovered a consistent path of superior human performance leading to profitable growth.

Here's what a manager who oversees more than three thousand employees in more than one hundred teams had to say. She believes her most successful teams got to be that way because of the emotional engagement of the employees along with the artful work of their managers. This is a part of the path she says makes them so great:

> Their talent, and their inner belief system that a manager can suport, make a significant difference in an associate, a team, a company, and with clients. Money is a minimal motivator. The right money or pay focus matters more than how much. The other motivator is seeing their team win awards as individual achievers, or win center or location awards cumulatively for their combined performances.

When asked how her best managers created and sustained this level of employee engagement, she said:

> By sincerely listening and caring about what makes each individual "tick" to help push them to new heights of performance, and consequently, retention and engagement. Also . . . by encouraging and creating teams that build off each other and create multiplicity and lifelong friendships, versus a bunch of individual achievers who care only about themselves.

Then take the example of the vice president for human resources at a very successful medical equipment manufacturing corporation—an organization that has achieved consistent double-digit growth over fifteen years. He attributes this growth to the manner in which his company selects and then develops the unique strengths of every individual employee:

Gallup: What do you trust as a predictor of individual superior performance?

Well, I was taught to always look at the experience of the individual, but I have found that this is not always a reliable predictor. I guess the correct answer is, "It depends"—on the specific role we are trying to fill. If we don't know what excellence is for every job, we cannot develop the road map to help us know what talents, skills, and experience we are looking for. As an example, when we are trying to fill a job in marketing communications, we know that it requires a "critical eye" to ensure that the final document perfectly lays out the features and application implications of our product. Some would call this perfectionism, but I call it an internal yearning for extreme accuracy and the ability to see the communication from the users' perspective. They are always asking "what if?" and anticipating the next question that comes to the reader's mind.

On the other hand, if I am seeking a top-notch sales manager, I look for that natural ability to "set the bar high" and then demand results to meet this standard. But we also know that our best sales managers do this through the development of very strong communication and relationships with those close to the action. They possess a natural ability to see the potential of every person they manage, and do everything possible to help the person be successful. Our great sales managers are very performance oriented, and when their people's performance is not at the level it should be, they act quickly and reposition the person to another role (inside or outside the company). They *never* lower the bar and settle for anything but excellence in performance.

Gallup: What do you look for in an applicant?

Once again, it depends on the role. I look for those who possess natural abilities like our best. I always let our stars (in every role) set the formula for the talents we are looking for. This may appear simple, but it is not. It starts with a fundamental shift in the traditional HR paradigm. Traditionally, HR has filled roles with the most convenient traits (willingness to relocate, industry experience, ability to start quickly, agreement to pay plan, etcetera) versus the "right" talents. We in HR have been taught to "limit risk" wherever possible, and this has forced us to be able to clearly identify those blatant characteristics that we don't want, versus keeping the standards high and knowing clearly what we do want. We have a very structured interview that gives us a nonbiased insight into the individual's natural strengths, and then we match those up against our best and see how they stand against our best in each job classification.

Gallup: How do you develop the strengths of your employees?

Well, it starts by realizing that development is not a strategic initiative. It is a local, close-to-the-action responsibility of every manager and employee. It starts with helping every new employee know exactly why they were hired. It begins day one. The specific talents and skills of the associate identified in the selection interview are shared with both the manager and associate, and dialogue begins. Our managers know that they have to be active in the feedback about how they see their direct reports playing on their strengths every day. Managers point out excellence as it occurs and are always trying to build self-awareness in the employee. See, selection of employees is really about if they can do the job very well; development is about how they will use their special strengths to achieve the outcomes of the role. We have literally been able to save tens of millions of dollars by cutting out remedial training that has been inappropriately labeled "development" because it has shown no return on investment.

And here's what a CEO had to say. The following interview was with a leader of one of the most profitable corporations in the United States. During his leadership, the stock value of his company has grown tenfold in a period of ten years. Every year his company has managed to produce double-digit increases in growth and profitability.

Gallup: What do you get paid to do?
Increase the stock value of this corporation.

Gallup: What is the biggest challenge you face today?
In today's business world there are only two possible challenges for people like me. One is to reduce costs more—and thereby cut prices—and the other is to grow margins by acquiring and sustaining profitable customers. I am a member of this second group.

Gallup: Why aren't you a member of the first group?
Because there is no sustainable future in that group. We are just kidding ourselves if we think that our stock growth strategy is realistically sound if we just reduce costs or prices. It's now very simple for anyone to do anything even more cheaply. The time has come when we must do something else.

Gallup: What do you mean by "something else"?
The value of our stock will only grow as a consequence of profit increases that are driven by real customer growth, not just by reducing costs.

Gallup: What is the basis of your strategy?

Let me begin with a question. What percent of our time and our resources do we currently spend in creating demand, just attracting any new customers? Compare that with the percent we spend on targeting and retaining profitable customers. My success story lies in doing one thing extremely well, and that is creating and cultivating strong relationships with my very profitable customers, value that exceeds good prices and good products, one customer at a time.

Gallup: How do you do that?

Actually, I don't do it. I can't. It's the employees of this company who do it, every single one of them, every single day. We have been fortunate to see that it is at the level of a personal interaction with our customers where we can establish a bond strong enough to rise above price and the usual product and service quality stuff.

Gallup: How do you know and how do you manage it?

By numbers, just like everything else.

Gallup: How do you know it works?

We do more with the same people, we earn more with the same customers, and we are very, very good at it. We do it uniquely fast.

Gallup: What path do you follow?

Emotional engagement, both for employees and for customers.

The Steps to Follow

In this book we're going to show you how the steps of the path are formed, how they link together, and why it is inevitable that they fit together so seamlessly. Together they form a bridge that will take you from the old, insular way of operating, full of its fluctuations and inconsistencies, to a revolutionary new way of functioning where healthy growth can be built and maintained.

An *emotion-driven economy* has infinite horizons. If your organization dreams of not merely surviving but actually thriving in tough times; if it acknowledges that doing things the tried-and-true way is now tired and through; if it wants to make itself great, but fears it will never know how, it is time to change directions.

Once you see how smooth the path is—how it avoids the detours of counterproductive practices and the ravines of self-defeating traditional ways of making use of employees and retaining customers—you will want to follow it, too. The amazing thing about the path is that it expands as it is traveled, allowing more people to use it. It leads directly to the destination every organization sets off to find: sustained growth and increased profitability. To make sure you get there, too, a map for traveling on the path is provided, and directions for managers are included.

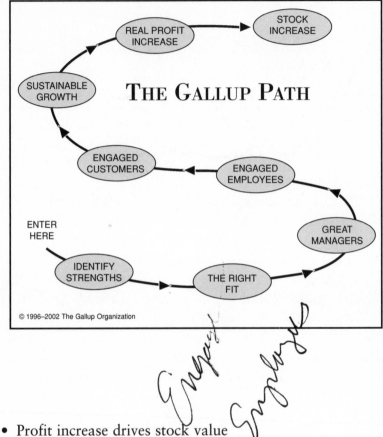

- Profit increase drives stock value
- Real sales growth drives profit increase
- Engaged customers drive sustainable growth
- Engaged employees create engaged customers
- Great managers transform talented individuals into engaged employees
- Roles fitting talent create talented individuals

CHAPTER 1

Welcome to the Emotional Economy

One Man's Vision

One day in 1609 Galileo stood on his balcony, peered at his world in a new way, and changed it. What he used to achieve this milestone was actually very simple. He took implements that were readily available to him—a piece of organ pipe fitted with a curved lens at either end—and gazed through it.

Pointing his telescope toward the rippling ocean, he saw what no one else could. Two ships far off, their billowing sails driven by a steady wind, aimed their bows directly at him. A magnified world, he realized, had enormous practical possibilities. Enemies could be spotted before they readied for attack. Friendly vessels, long away from home and feared lost, would be "there" before they docked. This was an innovation that people could understand—and they embraced it.

Then he shifted his focus from the world he knew. Turning his implement to the vast seventeenth-century sky once again, he saw something that no one else could. Peering at the magnified heavens, Galileo discovered four small moons circling the huge mass of Jupiter. Dark spots on the sun's bright surface were suddenly visible, as was the now illuminated surface of the moon as the sun's rays reached it.

These celestial bodies, he realized, were moving. But why?

The prevailing theory of Galileo's time held that the earth was the center of the universe. The spheres surrounding it were supposed to move as a group, not as independent entities.

Galileo knew that his findings were consistent with a view radically different from the accepted wisdom. Copernicus had already put forth the radical idea that the earth actually revolved around the sun, and not the other way around. Galileo also knew that expressing beliefs contrary to rock-solid dogma could be deadly: In 1600 Giordano Bruno, a Dominican friar, had been burned at the stake in Rome because he had insisted that the earth did not remain motionless at the center of the universe.

Obviously, a different perspective on the accepted world they inhabited terrified a lot of the good people of the time. Unlike the ocean view through the telescope, which brought the objects of their world "closer," this sky revelation created chaos. What did this information mean? How could they deal with it? Could it hurt them? Would they have to change the way they lived? The familiarity of their world was being questioned, and there didn't seem to be any ready answers. So instead of trying to understand the message of the spheres, they punished the messengers who delivered the "bad" news.

It took a long time, but eventually Galileo's keen observations changed our understanding of how natural forces operate in the universe. Back on earth, they altered how the planet itself was viewed and linked it into the bigger picture of space. Without this knowledge astronauts could not have traveled to the moon.

With a symbolic step into the unknown, Galileo helped create a path to a world he could not have imagined.

A New World's Old Way to Look at Business

Today's visible business world is not unlike the world in which Galileo lived. Many innovations—like technology— are embraced as long as they don't shake up long-established foundations. Machines are controllable and fixable. What they can and can't do is well understood, and how they affect business is usually highly appreciated.

But the other system that fuels business—human nature—is a whole other matter. Humans are emotion-driven entities, and emotions are messy. Little understood and less than predictable, emotions can disrupt, cause upheavals, and occasionally inspire fear. Certainly this ever-present human aspect is regarded as an annoying hindrance, something to be glossed over or avoided altogether. Think about it. Have you ever had to manage:

- Judy, "the thinker," who seems to spend hours staring into space?
- Ed, "the always excited," who can't restrain himself from leaping into every new project with gung-ho abandon?
- Raphael, "so quiet you don't know he's there," who turns in precision work?
- Stephanie, "the caretaker," who spends too much time remembering when people started work and commemorating the occasion with a cake?
- Ralph, "the boss-in-training," who wants to head every committee?

These kinds of employees (and there are lots more) get under your skin. You don't want to deal with their quirks and tics and habits because you believe they take precious time away from work.

Unfortunately, your view is upside down. All those personal "tics" are clues to who these people are—and, more important, to the innate talents they possess.

Just as the prevailing "wisdom" in Galileo's time forbade changes in what was accepted as true, businesses today tend to turn a blind eye to a force they don't want to understand because they don't know how to deal with it. Nor do they comprehend what it means to them.

THE ANTI-EMOTIONAL BELIEF SYSTEM

It's time to toss aside the antiquated "rules" of management, and for a good reason: They don't work.

Consider the tenets of the accepted wisdom regarding employees:

- Everyone can excel at anything provided they try hard enough.
- People will work harder only if they get paid more and are given perks.
- The focus of employees' development should be on fixing their weaknesses.
- An organization's outcomes are dictated by the hard financial realities of better products and processes, not people.
- Treat every employee the same way.
- The key to growth is increasing demand.
- Superior performance is the result of improved technology.
- Competencies, skills, and knowledge are always more important than talent.
- Superior performance is the consequence of rational thinking, so emotions should not be allowed to affect reason.
- "People" are an organization's most valuable asset.

> *And where customers are concerned,*
> *the beliefs can be summarized like this:*
>
> - Customers "know" what they want: better products at reasonable prices that will keep them coming back for more.
> - Customers are always right; just give them what they want.
> - Treat every customer the same way.

This skewed view of human nature is as backward as the narrow view of the universe was in the 1600s, for a fundamental reason: It doesn't begin to consider how human nature can impact positively on business outcomes.

A growing number of executives intuitively know that their organizations are running at a fraction of their human potential. (They're right. It's less than one-third. This startling number, and many others like it, will be covered in detail later in this book.) They are aware of constant fluctuations in the job performance of individuals and teams. The behavior of customers, they realize, is not something that can be relied on. But just as Galileo wondered why the sky moved but didn't understand what drove it, these executives don't have at their disposal a way of describing, much less linking, their observations and finding a solution to their problem.

That's because most businesses regard the subjects of the "impact of people" and "human potential" as interesting issues in theory that are irrelevant to their organizations' financial outcomes in reality. The general assumptions are that these issues don't exert an important influence, so why bother understanding them?

The same head-in-the-sand viewpoint applies to customers. Organizations are well aware that enormous growth potential lies in existing customers rather than from new ones. In his popular book *The Loyalty Effect,* Frederick F. Reichheld notes that the result of turning 5 percent of ordinary customers into return ones leads to an average increase in profit per customer of between 25 and 100 percent. But while most organizations maximize their ability to attract new customers, they minimize their understanding of what makes these essential people come back over and over again.

What many organizations don't see—and what many don't want to understand—is that employee performance and its subsequent impact on customer engagement revolve around a motivating force that is determined in the brain and defines the specific talents and the emotional mechanisms everyone brings to their work.

But at the same time we are finally seeing a growing awareness of just how influential human nature is in determining business outcomes. Human nature, the "soft side" of an organization, is attracting interest, particularly in the financial community. Investment bankers are already studying "human capital," because they are realizing how important an issue it is for them. Recently, Piper Jaffray, the equity investment arm of U.S. Bancorp, issued a report entitled *Human Capital: Optimizing Talent in the Knowledge Economy,* which stressed the growing value of talented employees.

Leading accounting firms are also looking at human-related issues as being part of an organization's assets, not its liabilities. Customer reliability and brand equity are areas of special interest in this regard.

Across all kinds of organizations, references to "human capital" are growing. What does this term mean? It varies. Definitions include "the knowledge worker," "the talent pool," "the competent workforce," "the educated employee," and the more encompassing "enthusiastic workforce."

By whatever name, these references reflect a new alertness to the profound impact of human nature in the workplace.

Multinational organizations, such as the European Commission, have been studying the economic implications of human capital, and not just in terms of percentages of GDP (gross domestic product) invested in education (as Nobel laureate economist Gary Becker has advocated). They are examining the harder-to-measure implications of talent and employee involvement in the workplace. The common goal is this: to find the code of human nature's role in shaping a company's business outcomes.

There *is* a way to do this. Great organizations are keenly aware of it. They tap into the power of human nature every day. It is what makes them great.

The Unique Pathway

> *"Roads with the most traffic get widened. The ones that are rarely used fall into disrepair."*

What do roads have to do with business, much less human nature?

Everything.

Dr. Harry Chugani, professor of pediatrics, neurology, and radiology at Wayne State University School of Medicine, made the statement above in reference to synaptic connections in the brain, the pathways that have led to your individual talents from the day you were born.

That day every neuron in your brain sent out many thousands of signals. The purpose of this was to establish connections with other neurons in order to communicate with them. By the time you were three years old, each of your brain's one hundred billion neurons formed up to fifteen thousand of these connections.

But these created a problem. Now your young brain was being inundated with information, and not all of it could be understood. In order to make sense of this excess of data, over the next ten years or so your brain refined and refocused its network of connections. Stronger synapses grew. Weaker ones withered away. By the time you were fifteen these choices, determined by genetics, brain physiology, and environment, shaped high-speed communication among neurons. Rapid access to memory and information, fast learning and knowledge acquisition, emotional response mechanisms, and a particular framework for the interpretation of experience: All these systems were firmly established. The solid foundation of these building blocks formed your unique sense, the way you, as an individual, react to the world.

This, great organizations know, is the basis of the particular talents you bring to everything you do.

For instance, if your brain highway has strong connections for communication, you will be able to teach others around you rather complicated issues that can be translated into understandable stories. Or, on the other hand, if you work with someone who is forever saying the wrong thing at the wrong time to the wrong person, he is not acting out of malice. His communication connection is weak; he can't find the words to connect to the level of the person he is communicating with. Customer service is obviously not the place for him. Likewise, another person's brain will send her the right word time after time in the heat of a debate while a colleague will suffer word deprivation at the most critical moments. Obviously, the second person is better suited to dealing with customers than the first.

This is borne out by the work of University of Pennsylvania psychologist Martin Seligman, who has devoted much of his career to the study of what can be learned and unlearned. In his book *What You Can Change and What You Can't: Learning to Accept Who You Are,* he writes that an individual can change his opinions and preferences—but the manner in which he perceives the world around himself cannot be changed.

Furthermore, recent discoveries in neuroscience reveal that talent and better-quality performance involve not just the frontal lobes—the decision-making brain circuitry that houses intellect—but also the amygdala. The circuits that color experiences with emotions reside in this almond-shaped structure; anytime action trumps reason, your amygdala is working overtime. Thanks to these recent discoveries, we know that emotions are indispensable for adequate rational thinking.

In his book *How the Mind Works,* Massachusetts Institute of Technology psychologist Steven Pinker notes that emotions are the mechanisms that set the brain's highest-level goals. Once generated toward a favorable activity, an emotion triggers a "cascade of sub-goals that we call thinking and acting with no sharp line dividing thinking and feeling." In other words, emotions drive our reactions, which, in turn, are ruled by the innate talent we possess and our propensity to be emotionally engaged. Our natural predispositions explain our distinctive experiences.

Studies of top performers show something even more remarkable. When forced by a situation to make a split-second decision to operate at top speed, or when faced with the pressure of doubt, top performers report something distinctive. They say that a part of them feels several steps ahead of what is going on. This helps them take control and anticipate possible alternatives for action. Where to pause, stop, and go is part of the package. Talent is their guide. Scientists use the world "supra-conscious" to describe this.

So there it is: Superior performance is not the exclusive product of the rational mind, no matter how appealing it is to business to believe this is so. Talent does intelligence one better, because it combines and utilizes the full circuitry (rational and emotional) of the brain's neural connections in the endless pursuit of a productive outcome.

Quality performance does, of course, require knowledge and skills—but talent makes it happen. And while individuals always operate in conditions of uncertainty (another fact that gives companies the jitters), their talent is an unsinkable life preserver. As long as it is acknowledged and utilized, innate talent always comes through, helping employees make better decisions and achieve finer results. In essence, talent and engagement are emotionally driven. In tough economic times, talent and emotional engagement are the only natural competitive advantages.

In his book *Synaptic Self,* reviewing the neurobiology of emotions, Joseph LeDoux, professor of science at New York University's Center for Neural Sciences, notes that "In spite of the tremendous similarity of our brains, we all act differently, have unique abilities, and have distinct preferences, desires, hopes, dreams, and fears. The key to individuality therefore, is not to be found in the overall organization of the brain, but rather in the fine tuning of the underlying networks."

Is it any wonder that great organizations make use of the brain's natural pathways? They are the reliable roads to continued success.

Reason and Emotion: It's a Chemical Reaction

Have you ever wondered why you prefer to watch the news on a certain television channel? Or why your kids "must" eat one special cereal morning after morning? Or why your family chooses to return to one resort year after year?

In the past, customer choices were regarded as being rational. Now we know something new. Emotions, to a very large degree, determine what customers respond to, what they buy—and what they keep returning to.

However, just as sight was not considered a legitimate proof of evidence in Galileo's time, emotions have long been regarded as elusive, "a baggage of evolution," subjective and almost impossible to measure objectively. For more than a century reason and emotion have been considered to be independent of one another. Reason has been viewed as the predominant characteristic of human beings, while emotions have been seen as the weaker human trait. Because of this, many people believed that reason could oppose and control emotion. How could someone be both rational and emotional? It just didn't make sense.

Emotions are the mechanisms of the mind least understood by management. Still, organizations have tried to trigger emotions by using all types of symbols—brands, products, and technology—and spending millions on advertising that appeals to the senses. But the least applied and the most power-ful transmitters of emotions are human beings. And of all the sources of emotional stimuli, the human voice and face are the most effective emotional markers. Every human interaction either elevates or downgrades the emotional state of a human being.

Recent discoveries in neuroscience and psychology bear this out. Neuroscience shows that emotional processes are integral to learning, reasoning, and decision making. It is now well accepted that much of what a person learns happens outside of conscious awareness.

And finally, it is clear that there is nothing vague, elusive, or mystical about emotions. Thanks to research discoveries and technological advances, emotions can now be observed and defined objectively as specific and consistent collections of physiological responses.

The process is immediate and direct. When a person receives a signal—for instance, she sees or hears something—a signal travels from her senses to her brain's emotional systems, which trigger a chemical reaction that in turn produces a feeling. It might be pleasant, such as happiness, surprise, pride, or excitement; or unpleasant, such as fear, sadness, anger, disgust, embarrassment, or guilt. Feelings are triggered by mechanisms that cannot be controlled. *All this happens without any conscious or rational intervention.*

Moreover, psychology has begun to show that emotions are required for superior performance in any occupation. Neuroscientist Antonio R. Damasio, in his book *The Feeling of What Happens,* shows that emotions point us to the sector of the decision-making space where our reason can operate most efficiently. His discoveries have led him to believe that "well-tuned and deployed emotion is necessary for the edifice of reason to operate properly."

Discoveries in neuroscience strongly suggest that emotions triumph over reason. Although thoughts can trigger emotions, our human mind is not very effective at willfully turning off emotions. Neural pathways from the brain structures that command our emotional responses (that is, the amygdala) to the brain systems that control our thoughts are wider and stronger than the pathways the other way around. So three central questions emerge: What are the right emotions that great organizations promote in every employee and every customer—the ones that systematically lead to engagement and growth? What are the mechanisms that these organizations employ to generate these emotional responses? And finally, how do they systematize these practices to make them universal within the organization as a whole?

A response to these three questions is what The Gallup Path leads to, again and again. Emotional engagement is the fuel that drives the most productive employees and the most profitable customers. As you travel along The Gallup Path with us, you will be amazed at just how powerful emotional fuel is. The most amazing thing about it is that it never runs out.

Emotions Are a Terrific Thing to Value

Here's what the world's most successful organizations *don't* do. They don't suppose that either superior college grades or comprehensive training is the only accurate or dependable indicator of the right person for the right job. Neither do they expect that employee incentives will guarantee consistently better job performance.

Instead they depend on the reliable source that other businesses disdain: *human nature*. They know that the emotions of both employees and customers create feelings, which drive their behavior. Great organizations are aware of the power of emotions and therefore set up the conditions that generate and cultivate emotional mechanisms among employees and customers. The only way to achieve this is through human interaction, the fastest and most powerful trigger of emotional states.

By recognizing and unleashing the innate abilities of employees and matching their gifts to the positions that will best take advantage of them, thus making them even stronger, great organizations look inward in order to move forward.

They cherish the fluctuations in human behavior because they understand that these create a pathway as electric as any inside a brain:

- Employees who use their natural talents in their jobs produce significantly more than average workers.
- Emotionally committed employees form teams that deliver exceptional outcomes.
- Customers recognize the passion and commitment employees feel toward them and cannot help but respond in an emotional way.
- This emotionally driven reaction builds a bridge between employees and customers that creates engagement.
- This engagement becomes the key factor that drives sustainable growth.
- Sustainable growth is the route to profits and, ultimately, higher stock value.

In the end great organizations know that a reason-driven economy can travel only so far. The missing link is the engagement of deep-seated emotions as the driver of growth and profits. These—and only these—feelings are the fuel that propel talented individuals to do more, and inspire customers to return. And while reason influences both employees and customers, emotions are indispensable because they drive the best in both of them. Finally, a chemical reaction inside the brain can be converted into a business model that works.

EMOTIONS DRIVE BUSINESS OUTCOMES

If you want to open the gate to the pathways that lead to greater profits and growth, you must change the way you view emotions in terms of your employees and your customers. These people are a lot more complicated than you think. If you want to understand what makes them tick, those forces that drive their actions and reactions, you must understand the role that emotions play in their behavior. The implications of the effects of emotions both inside and outside the workplace are incredibly powerful and far reaching. Emotions:

- Set the highest-level goals, including how hard a person works and how attached a person will stay to a brand or to an organization.
- Take place outside the rational, willful awareness and constitute emotional memory.
- Drive decision making, the emotional state of conscious awareness.

By acknowledging the role emotions play in driving business outcomes, you have taken the first step on The Gallup Path.

CHAPTER 2

Discover the Talents of Each Employee

The Blooming Rose and the Fault Line

Mike Rose is great at what he does, and it shows. Leaning back in his chair, his feet resting on his desk, headphone in place, he inhabits his area—he refers to it as the "command center"—with ease. Relaying information and answering questions with an enthusiastic manner that is endlessly engaging to the people on the other end of the line, Mike enjoys his job. When speaking to customers, he exhibits what seems to be a magical ability to "read" them, even though he never sees them.

Information technology is Mike's field of operation. He interacts with established and potential customers, presenting new products and services to them. Providing technical support is another part of his work.

But for Mike, the very process of speaking to people, finding out their likes and dislikes, guiding them to the products and services that are right for them—that's what gets him psyched every morning:

I have the best time talking to people and figuring out what is or isn't important to them. When I make a connection, I hear it in their voices, and it makes me feel good.

When asked how he performs such sleight of hand—Mike has developed quite a reputation as Mike the Magician—he shrugs his shoulders:

Beats me. I get a big charge out of turning dissatisfied customers into people who want to stay with us. And my day is made when I bring a new customer in.

Mike's connection with the people he speaks to is emotional.

Tom Fault, who sits a couple of rows away from Mike, looks over at his colleague, tries to relax his tight shoulders, and sighs. He doesn't understand it; he and Mike put in the same training time. He is as technically competent as Mike and longs to perform as well as he does. And he tries: Reminders of the basic customer tenets (these include active listening, communicating concern, paraphrasing the problem back, identifying the party at fault and the severity of the problem) are taped to his bulletin board. He mentally reviews the means of quickly assessing particular customer characteristics, grouping them in terms of their level of technical sophistication and specific needs, before each call. Then, of course, he knows the basic rules that everybody is supposed to follow:

- Always smile when you talk to customers, even if they can't see you.
- The customer is always right.
- Provide complete information; that's the way to fulfill a customer's expectations.
- Treat customers right.

So Tom has a tough time understanding why his intense preparations and fervent wish to succeed aren't working:

I try to sound friendly and courteous, just as I was taught to be. But for some reason I can't fathom, when I pick up the phone everything falls apart. I forget the client's name. Somehow I naturally arouse their frustration and anger. Basically, I lose the person as soon as I say hello. It's terribly demoralizing. I just don't get it. Mike and I have been here the same number of years and he is bringing in new customers while I'm losing old ones.

Tom is not able to connect to customers emotionally.
Mike and Tom differ in a very crucial way. Mike has a natural talent for his work, which comes to him easily. He doesn't "sweat" it. Certainly he has been trained, so he has the skills he needs. But he brings something else, something that cannot be taught. When he connects with customers, he feels good. They, in turn, feel that he cares about them. Consequently, Mike's work keeps blooming into profits.

Tom, on the other hand, just doesn't have a natural predisposition for the job he wants to do well. This truth comes across subliminally to customers, who react badly to him. Tom's work is a fault line that shakes up the bottom line.

The longer Tom toils away at a job not suited to his particular talents, the more the customer base erodes. He just can't work to full capacity in the job he's in. Sadly, maybe he knows what he is really good at and doesn't think it counts (although realistically assessing Mike could make him rethink this point of view). Or perhaps he doesn't believe that he could ever have the opportunity to be at his best, so he muddles through at what he doesn't do particularly well.

In Tom's case an even bigger attempt to try to motivate customers could be undertaken. But if after years of trying, with every good intention, he's still not able to perform as well as Mike does, how realistic and how cost effective is it to try to remake him into something he isn't?

Phoning It In

Mike and Tom are real people. They are part of a workforce of millions who make their living through the phone. They are just two examples of the wide range of performance that exists in call centers all over the world. The influence that extends from each person picking up a phone and representing his company is nothing short of staggering.

Gallup's research shows that the most effective employees are powerful brand boosters, while the least effective force customers to seek solace with competitors. For instance, one large company, with multiple call centers, sees that its top 1 percent of performers create engagement among an amazing 88 percent of customers they talk to. The top-achieving 5 to 10 percent of employees also earn very respectable engagement numbers. The top seven employees, however, ace each conversation: They enhance engagement with every customer they speak to.

If you look at the same company's worst performance numbers, the results are equally dramatic—and a lot more troubling. Employees who reduce engagement by 14 percent after speaking to customers are considered the bottom 10 percent. They destroy more loyalty than they create. After them, the bottom 5 percent—employing rudeness, insensitivity, and the consistent inability to solve problems—cause engagement to plunge even more. The three worst employees are in a class unto themselves. They manage to eradicate customer allegiance completely.

What could account for this kind of dramatic discrepancy within one company?

Gallup asked millions of employees in sixty-six countries this question: "*Do you get the chance to do what you do best at work every day?*" The answers were sobering and eye-opening. Only one in five—a mere 20 percent—said yes. Think of it this way. Imagine a bank where twenty of its one hundred branches are open for business when they need to. Or an automobile manufacturer that makes millions of cars, but only 20 percent of them steer properly. Consider what would happen to a utility company if only 20 percent of its customers paid their bills.

The stunning reality is that most organizations see superior results from only 20 percent of their employees. In an attempt to fix the other 80 percent, they take a detour that keeps them in mediocreland.

Great Performance Can't Be Taught

Most organizations assume that anyone can excel in any job, provided they receive enough training and try hard enough. Tom Fault is just one example that shows the fallacy in that thinking.

Second, they take strengths for granted and try to fix weaknesses. This "competency" approach is a huge waste of energy and time, no matter how well intended, designed, and executed it is. The reason is simple: It is based on three flawed assumptions:

1. Those who excel in the same role all display the same behaviors.
2. Each of these behaviors can be learned.
3. Each of these behaviors should be learned, because improving weaknesses leads to success.

This accepted way of regarding employees derives from a long-held competency-building tradition. Because of this, training is focused on identifying which abilities employees are lacking and then trying to fill in these unfortunate gaps.

STAFF
DEV,
MODEL

Therefore, an employee's "area for improvement" is a not-so-subtle euphemism for her "area of weakness."

Jane, a front-line bank teller, expressed it this way:

> I feel that I'm under a microscope, that all my flaws are being sought all the time. Any weak spot is highlighted and kept for examination. This process doesn't help me. On the contrary, all it makes me feel is that I'm not capable enough, as if telling me this will change anything. I was hired, I thought, for what I could do—not what I couldn't.

Those employees who do manage to improve are rewarded, with either a promotion, a good raise, or a bigger bonus. But all this does is reinforce the company line that *how* employees get their work done is just as important as *how much* they accomplish. In order to keep this plan in place, management systems use these practices:

- Define the behavioral competencies expected in each role.
- Design interviewing methods that select employees with these specific behaviors.
- Once employees are hired, determine how they measure up to the accepted competencies.
- Identify the missing abilities. Label them something like "development needs" or "areas for improvement."
- Sit down with the employees, point out which competencies are lacking, and design an "individual development plan," which encourages them to "work on" and therefore improve those glaring flaws.
- Rate the person's progress on how they've mastered each competency. If improvement is shown, bestow a reward of a higher performance rating.

The competency approach is very popular with human resource departments because its explicit aim is to "develop people" and "build human capital." Human resources, therefore, becomes a "strategic partner" by adhering to the official list of desired competencies. This places human resources in a defensive, rather than an offensive, position.

While it is true that examples of employees who "worked on" their deficiencies for six months and showed some progress do exist, these "improvements" don't mean much. The competency approach is a dead end. It rarely succeeds in measurably improving either productivity, customer satisfaction, employee engagement or retention, or safety or performance records, all of which are the real measures of how effectively a person works.

THE WRONG WAY TO GO

Organizations continue to implement several wrong-minded decisions about employees that profoundly impact operations.

The first misstep is in the selection process, because it doesn't address what talents are needed to fill a position, much less the talents people bring with them. Instead, the concentration is on what is accepted as being important. But just how those "important" factors apply to the role offered is a mystery.

Take a look at employee ads; all the evidence you need is right there. A sample ad for a salesperson might request three years' experience and a university degree from a self-starter. Or if that isn't general enough, what about an ad for a brand manager that asks for an MBA, two years' experience in marketing, and the ability to work under pressure? Then there's the search for a product manager who should be a business school graduate, be dedicated to the job offered, and own a car. There is nothing wrong with stating the basics. What's wrong about this picture is that most companies end their selection process there. The only thing they look at is the résumé, not the person and his or her talent and strengths. It is assumed that everyone with the same background has the exact same potential for superior performance at a given role.

The second misstep is evaluation, a circular process that, like the parade in Alice in Wonderland, *ends up going nowhere.* So much time is spent concentrating on what a person doesn't bring to the job—after being hired to do it!—that frustration on behalf of managers and employees alike is the inevitable result. Instead of evaluating what a person shows strength in, and building on those strengths, the accepted idea is to ignore the good stuff and concentrate on the less-than-good. It's like being hired as a pitcher and then being told to concentrate on your hitting.

In the standard evaluation process, individual strengths are taken for granted, while "gaps" must be corrected. That means more training. If the training doesn't work the first time, then it can always be given again. And again.

The third misstep is training. Being sent to learn something for which they have little interest or aptitude is not a good use of either employees' or trainers' time. Receiving extra training to augment strengths is rarely considered. After all, why make better what already works? Instead, employees are directed to bolster those areas where they do not excel. To do this, organizations adhere to a strict regimen that is sadly familiar:

- Training is nearly indiscriminate, geared toward obtaining a common-denominator performance. The right training for the right person to maximize job performance isn't planned.
- Training is usually reduced to standardized information. That way, everyone has the same facts. Once

employees learn what they need in order to perform competently, the playing field—it is believed—will be leveled. A range in performance will disappear because everyone will function at the same acceptable level. But individuals vary—and so do the outcomes.

The fourth misstep is role allocation. Is there anyone who hasn't worked with a person who was promoted and then did an awful job in the new role? Because this person performed so brilliantly in a job that was so well suited to his strengths, he was given a new title, a new office, and, worst of all, a new position to fill. Unfortunately, what he did best was not pertinent to this exalted role. He suffered, as did his work and the people who reported to him.

In most organizations promotions are supposed to reflect accumulated knowledge and prestige. But in actuality talent is usually promoted to positions where it cannot shine. For instance, high-achieving salesmen who are moved up to management often fail at their new jobs. Promotion hurts them—and it damages the company they work for. In effect, this kind of promotion is a kind of punishment.

All these programs and policies only grind down an organization. The strong evidence collected by Gallup shows that a wide range of performance—a range that dramatically affects the financial basis of an organization—is a constant, despite a number of well-intentioned training activities.

Gallup has found that the only consistency involves the best performers. Their results create real and sustainable value.

Talent Is Where You Find It

What if technical innovations had stopped one hundred years ago and all subsequent inventions were based on one way of doing things? The world we know would not exist.

Where employees and talent are concerned, most organizations are operating as if it were the turn of the twentieth century. They still cling to the belief that high achievers are made, not born. If employees are simply given enough information (that is, knowledge) and trained long enough (in other words, are skilled), then they are bound to turn in high-quality work.

This approach is wrong. Neuroscience shows that everyone learns and does things according to the way they are hardwired. Therefore lessons, and the ability to apply them, come more easily to some than to others. And while organizations can widen the information highway accessible to employees, they can't change how the employees filter what they see along the way. The brain determines what information is used or ignored. No organization can alter this natural fact, not even if it spends millions of useless dollars trying to do so.

Great organizations know the difference between knowledge, skills, and talent. Knowledge is either factual, the information related to a job operation, or experiential, what is learned through experience. Knowledge and reason (conscious awareness) represent just a fraction of mental capabilities, particularly with regard to how emotions are awakened and stored. Skills are the nuts and bolts of a job, the "how-to" aspect, which comes with training. Talent, channeled through the right job, is the one constant required for superior performance.

A classic example of talent versus skills comes from economist and Nobel Prize winner Herbert Simon in an article he wrote back in 1972 entitled "Theories of Bounded Rationality." In an average chess game, he pointed out, the number of possible moves for a player equals 10 raised to the power of 120. This number is so far reaching that it would take more than a lifetime to make all the plays. Obviously, only a fraction of these potential moves will be put into play in any given game.

In a single game the players will know some of the possible actions they can take. A more seasoned player will likely remember more than someone new to the game. So with this information at hand, the "better" player should always win, because of her wealth of knowledge and accumulated skill. But chess doesn't work that way. A new adversary may come to the game with the natural gift of "seeing" plays, which translates into wins. Intelligence, it seems, is not the most reliable indicator of superior play. Talent, however, consistently is.

So just what *is* talent? Many people assume it is a special gift given only to a handful of people. They are the lucky ones, those who throw quadruple axels and win Olympic gold. They are the blessed music prodigies who coax heartbreaking sounds from violins with seven-year-old fingers. They are the moviemakers whose images crystallize the mood of a country in a single black-and-white frame.

They are the people with magic hands who can fix anything, from a toaster to a vintage T-bird. They are men and women who can organize and know where everything is and get it before it is needed. They are the people who can figure out where the red tape is and then find a way around it.

Talent is much more than this, however—and a lot more pervasive than is generally viewed. *Everyone* has talent—the natural predispositions that make each of us particularly effective. It is when this recurrent pattern of thinking, feeling, and behavior is applied to the right role that superior performance is generated. The trick is to find that role in which talents can be put to their best use.

Many organizations believe that talent is scarce, a rare, precious resource that comes along all too infrequently. Great organizations know that talent is an abundant resource waiting to be tapped.

Thirty-Four Routes to Superior Performance

Researchers at Gallup, led by Don Clifton and Marcus Buckingham, have provided us with the talent equivalent of a road map. Searching through mountains of data, they found thirty-four specific routes that lead to excellent performance. All of these nearly three dozen talent themes,* reflecting naturally recurring patterns of thinking, feeling, and behavior, include two distinct features that render them exceptional. First, they are created by the connections inside the brain. Second, they are enduring.

Our strong predominant neural pathways automatically guide our learning and trigger our emotional responses. The combination of top talents accounts for the particular potential for superior performance in an individual. Because every person is unique, some people will exhibit talents, to some degree, beyond their very dominant themes. Some won't.

It is important to note that while a person can possess a few or many of the themes within each category, it is the *combination and intensity* of these themes that render a person unique.

The thirty-four talent themes explain differences in terms of how people relate to one another, make an impact on others, strive toward goals, and think. They are thus divided into four main groupings: Relating, Impacting, Striving, and

*StrengthsFinder® and the thirty-four StrengthsFinder theme names are trademarks of The Gallup Organization, Princeton, New Jersey. All other trademarks are the property of their respective owners. Copyright © 2000 The Gallup Organization, Princeton, New Jersey. All rights reserved.

Thinking. Under these sections, specific types of talents are listed.

Relating Themes	Impacting Themes	Striving Themes	Thinking Themes
Communication	Command	Achiever	Analytical
Empathy	Competition	Activator	Arranger
Harmony	Developer	Adaptability	Connectedness
Includer*	Maximizer	Belief	Consistency†
Individualization	Positivity	Discipline	Context
Relator	Woo	Focus	Deliberative
Responsibility		Restorative	Futuristic
		Self-Assurance	Ideation
		Significance	Input
			Intellection
			Learner
			Strategic

*Previously "inclusiveness"
†Previously "fairness"

Everyone you've ever met has strengths determined by these themes—and you've reacted emotionally to every one of them. Let's meet some of them again, as they were in high school—and perhaps really get to know them for the first time.

RELATING TALENTS

Relating talents are contained in the themes used to effectively create, develop, and sustain relationships. These themes prompt how a person reaches out to others and responds to those who reach out to him. Relating talents differentiate how someone naturally forms personal relationships as well as demonstrating the unique means by which he creates new relationships and the pattern chosen for maintaining them.

The Relating themes are:

Communication

From the time she could talk, Sarah was popular because she was a great storyteller. In high school she was the captain of the debate team. She could take the driest topic and make it pop with colorful and fascinating facts.

The desire to explain, host, write, or speak in public is the hallmark of Communication. Breathing life into static ideas by turning events into stories draws people to listen.

Empathy

David could walk into a room and know how you were feeling that day. Whenever a new student arrived, he knew if she was feeling left out. He would always introduce himself to help her feel welcome.

Someone with Empathy can understand the emotions another person is experiencing, even though he doesn't automatically agree with those feelings. At the same time, while he doesn't become mired in the frustrations, anger, or sadness of another person, by using his "emotional radar" the empathic individual can interpret the shifting moods of someone moment by moment.

Harmony

Andrew couldn't stand conflict. Whenever he sensed a disagreement or a fight coming, he'd pay attention to what was being said, observe what was going on, and try to make peace by pointing out what both sides had in common.

Peacemakers, people with Harmony, turn the attention away from themselves and onto others. Often those with

Harmony are especially sensitive to the tones of people's voices, their moods, and the atmosphere in which they find themselves. Because little is to be gained from disagreement, it must be held to a minimum.

Includer

Every time Daniel hosted a party, more and more people showed up. Even after invitations were extended, he'd invite more people. The way he figured it, there was always a way to make room for one more person.

Inclusiveness is a philosophy of life. Making people feel that they belong is important, because everyone will benefit from the support of others.

Individualization

Amy's gifts were always welcome because she inevitably knew exactly what someone wanted.

People with Individualization ask the right questions to gather information and check out whether or not their hunches about someone's mood, talents, limitations, and so forth are correct. Good observers and listeners, they pick up insights and information that they can use later. Generalizations are dismissed, because the differences among people, the distinctive qualities that make each person special, are worth real attention.

Relator

Janie could always be seen with her tight-knit group of three close friends. They studied, ate lunch, and went to the movies together.

Being pulled toward people already known is the signature of the Relator. A deep relationship with a few cherished friends is much more important than having dozens of acquaintances. Nurturing close bonds with a few people is more important than calling everyone they meet "friend."

Responsibility

No matter how demanding the assignment, once Paul accepted it he would get it done. If the drama class needed ten green velvet costumes by Thursday, Paul would find them.

"Commitment" and "follow-through" are the bywords of those with Responsibility. Most tasks taken on, whether large or small, must be completed. Doing a job halfway is just not possible. Mediocrity, missing steps, or overlooking details is unacceptable. Dependability, the willingness to be held accountable rather than blame others, to be reliable and trustworthy: This is what someone with Responsibility is all about.

IMPACTING TALENTS

Impacting talents are contained in the themes used to motivate others to action. Talents within these themes prompt a person to set a course for individuals and groups to follow, then get them moving along that course. Those with Impacting talents stimulate others to be more productive, to reach for excellence, and to fulfill personal potential.

Impactors direct people toward their goals by helping them find the things they need to get there. Handing someone a book, for instance, wouldn't be a simple act of sharing. Rather, the specific book would contain information that the impactor felt the person needed to improve a situation or herself, or to provide necessary data or points of view. By filling such a requirement, the impactor can win over the other person. Impactors pay attention to people, although they don't necessarily befriend them.

Wherever they are, whatever they do, people with strength in Impacting themes make the most of it.

The Impacting themes are:

Command

Jessica was known as the General. She liked to run the concession stands at the football games because it gave her the chance to boss people around. Taking charge of a situation, forcing people to see her way of doing things, and not stopping until she got her way gave her a lot of satisfaction.

Not surprisingly, those with a taste for Command tend to take charge—and they experience no discomfort with imposing their "I'm going to get you to act" attitude on others.

Competition

"What grade did you get on your test?" was always Ronald's first question when papers were handed back. He'd think to himself, "I did better." Ronald's goal was to outscore everyone else.

Competition is rooted in comparison. Those who compete are instinctively aware of the performance of others—but their own actions are their ultimate yardsticks. Reaching a goal without outperforming peers is a hollow victory. It's always a thrill to face a risk with a specific reward in mind.

Developer

Pam was a mentor because she really believed in helping others achieve their potential. If you needed tutoring, she's the one you went to for help.

Developers see what could be and are drawn to people because every person is a work in progress. Helping individuals "grow" spurs growth in the Developer, too.

Maximizer

As the editor of the school paper, Howard strove for excellence. He picked the best interviewers, writers, and photographers, and his ad sales staff consistently bettered his budget. He even chose a more expensive printer because its finished product was superior to that of the less costly supplier. When the paper won the nation's top student newspaper award, Howard started looking for ways to improve upon an already outstanding publication.

Excellence, not mediocrity, is the measure of the Maximizer. After all, it takes just as much effort transforming something good into something superb, so why waste time trying to raise something average to slightly more than that? Strengths, no matter whom they belong to, are fascinating.

Positivity

When Elisa entered a room, she brought light in with her. "How are you?" were the first words she uttered when she saw someone she knew. Enthusiastic and encouraging, she always seemed to make things better. Also, she never forgot a birthday.

Generous with praise, quick to smile, the person with Positivity spontaneously looks for the good in others and in situations. Making the most of things, celebrating often; no wonder Positivity people are always surrounded by others. Spotlighting the people they encounter, they make others feel good, laugh, and have a good time. Their outlook boosts people's confidence, engenders feelings of warmth, and elevates sagging spirits.

Woo

Cindy always won others over; that's the definition of "Woo." A terrific campaigner, she built trust as soon as she shook someone's hand.

Meeting new people and getting their trust is what Woo is all about. Strangers, rarely intimidating, act as energizers. Concentrating on the person they want to like them or think well of them or feel better because of them: That's what the person with Woo seeks.

STRIVING TALENTS

Striving talents are contained in the themes utilized to push the self toward results. Talents within these themes motivate a person to get things done, then seek greater accomplishments. Striving talents can easily generate the energy needed to successfully complete even long-term projects, and to quickly move on to the next one.

Striving talents are the distinctive motivations that influence individuals to do the same task differently. These themes, called drivers, force people to get up each day and do something.

Strivers come in all kinds of categories. Some are self-starters, while others require an outside force to motivate them into action. Some live in a state of "compressed urgency"; they are impelled to make things happen ASAP. Thriving in ever-changing environments works for others. Some find their catalyst in a noble cause, a higher calling, or a core value.

A number of strivers blossom in highly organized, structured, or deadline-driven environments, but as many are single-minded and seldom lose sight of their main goal. Some naturally find people or things that need fixing, updating, or renovation. Others move forward because they trust themselves, while a number make progress because people acknowledge their successes, strengths, effectiveness, or importance. Striving themes are the fuel that propels people to excel, take risks, and set high expectations. Inaction renders them restless.

The Striving themes are:

Achiever

This was Robert, who was never satisfied with his high grades. His bar was always set high in order to get the results he wanted. Robert knew what he scored on the college entrance exams as soon as the test was over. Even as a sophomore he carried around a "to-do" list and checked off each goal as soon as it was accomplished.

A true Achiever harbors a deep need to accomplish something tangible in order to feel good about himself. This pushes him to do more, achieve more, and get those results.

Activator

Here's Jenny, known for her "that's enough talk; let's get going" attitude. If there was a theme for a school dance, Jenny was the one who launched it.

An Activator is impatient for things to happen. Her belief is that action, and only action, will make things happen.

Adaptability

Connie could adjust to unexpected changes in plans without a trace of anxiety. "Don't want to go to the basketball game? Okay! Want to go to a movie instead? Great!" was her inevitable attitude.

Adaptability means living in the moment, even if your plans get changed without warning. Change is a friend, never a foe.

Belief

When his neighbor's son was diagnosed with a serious illness and the family lacked the funds for treatment, Sam was the one who put together a fund-raiser—and worked hard to bring in enough money.

Seeking meaning and satisfaction by tapping into their core values, those with a strong theme for Belief don't measure success by either money or prestige. Rather, yearning to be part of activities that are considered to have a positive impact on the world is much more important. Commitment to family can be invaluable. Altruism, and being true to his ethics, is a big part of this person's makeup.

Discipline

Any teacher who had Beth in class knew better than to deviate from the lesson plan. And where deadlines were concerned, teachers knew that she would angrily voice her annoyance if she found out that a cutoff date was flexible. If a paper was due on Tuesday, Beth's was ready. Extensions were unnecessary.

For someone with Discipline, the world needs to be predictable, ordered, and planned. As a result, structure must be imposed, and routines followed. Timelines and deadlines make sense, because they aid in breaking down projects into specific short-term plans that can be worked on diligently.

Focus

Caroline always knew where she was going. She not only had her college picked out in her junior year but had already decided on what dorm she was going to live in, too, and how she was going to decorate her room.

A person with strong Focus has precisely defined goals and establishes measurable milestones to monitor her progress toward each objective. When unexpected obstacles or distractions pull her off course, as they will from time to time, the focused person quickly decides whether or not the problem warrants her attention. If it does, she will quickly deal with it. If it doesn't, she'll ignore it. Either way, the person with strong Focus wastes little time on activities that hinder her from concentrating on key goals.

Restorative

Todd spent his free time repairing and restoring a vintage bicycle he found in his grandparents' garage.

Excellent problem solvers, energized by problems that reduce others to tears—these are signs of the Restorative. Analyzing "symptoms," identifying what is wrong, and finding the solution is as good as life gets. Processes, plans, tactics, as well as objects and sometimes even people—all could be made better or improved.

Self-Assurance

Teachers and students alike turned to watch George when he walked down the hall. There was something about the way he carried himself. And then there was the way he spoke, with unwavering confidence. He didn't need outside praise to know he was capable.

An aura of quiet power—of certainty about themselves and their abilities—surrounds those with this theme. A self-assured individual trusts his judgment more than the judgment of others. He makes choices that suit him rather than setting out to win the approval of others.

Significance

Gloria campaigned for student government president and headed every committee she was on. Each time she outlined her accomplishments with ease.

Getting recognition—in the fullest sense of the word—guides those with strong Significance. Being heard, standing out in the crowd, being appreciated; someone with strong Significance believes she is noteworthy. That's why she will not associate herself with unimportant, average, or mediocre organizations, activities, or people. Whatever she allies with reflects upon her and she knows it.

THINKING TALENTS

Thinking talents involve the way people gather, process, and make decisions with information and mental images. Gallup research has shown that people spend the majority of their time thinking in either the past, the present, or the future. Those who dwell in the past are reliving experiences, trying to understand them and thus plan for what will happen in the future. Individuals who think in the moment also live in it. They respond to things as they occur. And those beings who think in the future explore the possibilities of what might happen. They find the thought of what's ahead not only challenging, but also extremely energizing.

In addition to thinking within a frame of time, those with these talent themes process information differently. Some take things apart in order to understand how they work. Others, like detectives, study data and search for evidence. Coordinating events, schedules, and projects comes easily to many of them, while some think globally, sensing they are linked with all of humankind past and present.

Others ponder issues or ideas for hours, days, or months before sharing an idea with anyone, while a number of them love to think out loud, testing their concepts or recommendations on either a friend, partner, group, or stranger. Solitude, in order to do their best thinking, suits a lot of thinkers. But while many bring a consistency to their thinking that makes them utterly predictable—what they say or do today is what they have been saying and doing for weeks, months, or even years—some generate innovative ideas. Looking at an opportunity, problem, person, process, or thing from many angles before drawing a conclusion can be part of the process, but some gather obvious insights from conversations, experiences, and books with no particular aim in mind. Thinkers can be philosophical by nature, delving deep into a problem, subject, or theory. Some are possibility thinkers, tacticians, or perpetual students.

However they exhibit it, people's Thinking themes definitely influence the way they view the world, treat others, interpret current events, solve problems, and create opportunities. Each Thinking theme gives people a unique perspective on themselves, others, and the world we all live in.

Thinking contains the themes used to analyze the world. Talents within these themes drive a person to logically approach a situation, think it through, and then plan accordingly. Using Thinking talents, a person "works smart" toward increased effectiveness, and leads others who are impressed with such thoroughness to do the same.

The Thinking themes are:

Analytical

Was there anyone who raised a hand more than Leonard? He challenged teacher after teacher, no matter what subject they were presenting. Inspiring his classmates to groan every time he waved his arm in the air, Leonard didn't accept rumors, either. "Facts, and nothing but the facts," was his personal credo.

Analytical people demand proof. "Show me how what you are claiming is documented and true" is their mantra.

Arranger

Mark was a born rethinker. "There's got to a better way" was his personal slogan. Were chairs aligned in rows? Mark would be the one to suggest that a class would be more fun and more could be learned if they were arranged in a circle instead.

When faced with complex situations involving many factors, Arrangers enjoy managing the variables. They delight in aligning and realigning until they are sure they have achieved the most productive configuration possible.

Connectedness

Around school Kate was known as the "old soul." Whenever something unexpected happened, she offered the same calm words: "I guess it was meant to be; everything happens for a reason." Considerate, caring, accepting: These words were always used to describe her.

Those with a talent for Connectedness can't be moved from their unwavering understanding that everyone is linked. This offers enormous comfort, because it confirms that people are not isolated from one another. It also means connected people sense that their words affect everyone else in some way, and vice versa.

Consistency

Ivy was the champion of "everyone should have a chance." Any athletic program geared to star players was a particular target. "Everyone should get to play—at least some of the time"—was her equitable solution.

On the great seesaw of life, those with a strong Consistency theme try to find balance. Everyone should be treated alike, no matter what they do or who they are. The consistent will guard against giving one person an advantage over everyone else.

Context

Josh loved history. Every field trip was an adventure, because it helped him to make sense of the present by looking at the past. Researching papers about historical figures was his idea of fun.

To those driven by Context, the past provides the blueprints of cause and effect. What already took place is the guide to understanding what is happening now.

Deliberative

Pete was the quintessential "what if?" guy. He wouldn't use a computer at school without backing everything up, because "what if there's a power surge?" Before he did anything he would sit down with paper and pen and evaluate all the benefits and risks associated with it.

Vigilance and being careful are the prime descriptions of the Deliberative theme. The world is an unpredictable place, so it makes sense to identify possible risks so that they can be identified, assessed, and ultimately reduced.

Futuristic

Brian spoke constantly about where he'd be in five or ten years. To the amazement of many of his fellow students, he was already envisioning the twenty-year reunion.

To be Futuristic means being fascinated with what is possible in the coming months, years, or decades. The strongly Futuristic person generates numerous options, assesses the situation, identifies the available resources—people, time, money, materials—and sorts them according to the one best alternative. Futurists ask two questions: "What if? . . ." and "What will happen if we do that?"

Ideation

"I have an idea: How about making this year's talent show retro, where everyone performing picks a decade and then performs to music from that time?" Tom was a treasure trove of innovative ideas; some of them were actually adopted by the school.

Innovative concepts, theories, and solutions are the essence of Ideation. People with strength in this talent theme find simple ways to explain most events. Where Ideation is concerned, basic concepts drive the most complicated matters. The delight is in finding that uncomplicated idea.

Input

A collector of train trivia, Fred searched for books and models, attending shows whenever he could. Gathering as much data as he could was a joy for him.

Additional information or ideas or things pertaining to their interest is especially valuable to people with strong Input, because they know that someday it will prove valuable. Being inquisitive and collecting represents how wonderfully complex and varied the world is.

Intellection

Emily had the right name, because, like her namesake Emily Dickinson, she was a deep thinker who liked to read poetry and then contemplate its meaning privately.

Being alone is precious because it allows time for musing and reflection. Intellection reflects the pleasure of thinking and figuring things out.

Learner

After-school classes were Sandy's steady habit. Tennis lessons, dance classes, Saturday afternoon sculpture— all thrilled her.

As the name suggests, strong Learners love the process of acquiring new information and/or skills, and do so throughout their lives.

Strategic

From the day Tony started high school, he planned how he was going to get a college scholarship. He realized that everything he did counted. That meant changing the kids he socialized with, so he made friends with boys and girls in the honors classes. He joined the debate team and did volunteer work because he knew it would look good on his college applications.

"What if?" and "Then what?" are the definers of those with a strong Strategic theme. They will generate numerous options; determine available resources, including people, time, money, and materials; assess a situation factually and logically; figure out the consequences of each option; and select and implement the best choice. Sifting through clutter and finding the most direct route marks the Strategic theme. Information gathering leads to understanding the issue at hand. Patterns emerge where others see chaos.

The Symphony Conductor and the NBA Player

Talent themes are the key sources of individual strengths— no matter what the job is. Consider these two seemingly diverse examples and note the specific talents in parentheses.

In the 1990s a very special request came to Gallup to study the talent of great symphony orchestra conductors. The information we gleaned was fascinating. Many conductors referred to being aware of music inside them from the time they were children and feeling a strong compulsion to express what they heard internally through playing an instrument, composing, or conducting. One said, "I always wanted to be a musician and then a conductor because you are in a position to influence the course of music" (*Learner, Focus,* and *Achiever*).

Many expressed their sense that music is good only when it is played at its best and true to the way the composer wrote it. To make this happen, they like to see their musicians develop their abilities as far as they can go (*Maximizer* and *Developer*). Often the conductors facilitate this process. Some conductors

use music as the conduit for their own emotions and attain actual spiritual pleasure by leading an orchestra. Intense joy and
personal satisfaction flow when they conduct the music they
love. Others are inspired by the deep sense of purpose they feel
when they interpret what they view as the finest music. Their
strong desire to make a major difference in the lives of others
through the music they perform is very dear to them.

But all great conductors are perfectionists, which demands a great combination of talents. The blend may include a deep understanding of a composer's intention
(*Belief*), a natural drive for excellence (*Maximizer*), taking
charge over the work of others (*Command*), a strong desire
to reach the audience (*Communication*), or an intense
yearning to gain recognition (*Significance*).

This combination of talent is the essential requirement
without which an orchestra cannot be brought to the height
of its potential. Never satisfied, conductors are obsessed with
endless improvement (*Maximizer* and *Achiever*). In their relentless drive toward excellence, they become intimidating,
self-centered, and domineering (*Command*). They are in control of their orchestra at all times.

The reason for this, they say, is that they feel blessed with
the capacity to interpret the works of great composers; there
is a direct link between the person who wrote the music and
themselves (*Maximizer*). Ultimately, they want to reach the
audience, and get them to feel what they call an "aesthetic
awareness" (*Connectedness* and *Belief*).

Making music is, to them, the most satisfying possible
profession, and they love what they do. As one said, "I can't
imagine myself living in this world without music. If I can
bring music through myself to other people, I am very happy
about it." (There's an emotional link if there ever was one).

Some time ago a National Basketball Association (NBA)
franchise approached Gallup with a very intriguing question:
What drives the performance of the top basketball stars? It

would seem that all the players had, in effect, an equal chance to excel. They had access to in-depth training and specialized treatments for injuries, and they arrived on the court with sophisticated skills honed by years of play. Physically, they were in prime shape. So why wasn't everyone playing the way coaches and owners expected them to?

The initial part of the study revealed some combinations of talent themes that were specific to certain positions. Successful centers, for instance, tended to have a strong *Focus* that often stressed winning. Point guards, in contrast, could easily mentally project images of plays and passes, which allowed them to slow the game down in their minds and make decisions (*Strategic, Maximizer,* and *Achiever*).

Power forwards were another story. Courageous and aggressive, they were more likely than their teammates to participate in the physical part of the game and get a big rebound when the game was on the line (*Self-Assurance, Command,* and *Activator*).

But the really startling discovery about who "made it" or not came down to just two theme combinations. The first concerned *Focus,* the ability of players to stay fixated on their goals both during and after the games. The second was the burning desire to be the best, rather than just living up to potential (*Significance, Maximizer, Competition,* and *Achiever*). These players are more apt to accept strict coaching, and they take practice time very seriously. Also, when these great athletes play, they don't think about the steps they are taking; they perform intuitively because their talent themes allow them to do so.

Don Clifton, the chief consultant attached to this project, analyzed one particular player whom he recommended to his NBA client. Don thought the candidate harbored great talent, but the client saw things differently. Namely, all he noticed was that the player was too heavy, too slow, and that he couldn't jump. But talent never lies. The player in question went on to become one of the top fifty players of all time.

Thirty-Four Ways to Discover Great Employees

If you know that the way employees are chosen is not working, there is a way to improve your selection process. It is possible to hire the right person for the right job. If you realize that stressing a person's weaknesses instead of bolstering her strengths isn't resulting in superior performance, there is a better way to manage the people in your work group. If you see that training is not getting you better workers, there is a way to direct training so that it is effective. And if you recognize that promoting people into jobs that they don't excel in doesn't do the person or the organization any good, it's time to change the way you manage.

After years of reviewing data, we know that working from a position of strengths is the most efficient way to use employees. That's why great organizations recognize the thirty-four unique and enduring talents and employ them to the best advantage.

THE RIGHT TALENT IS IN YOUR ORGANIZATION RIGHT NOW

It's time to stop looking at—and treating—your employees as you've always done. Your organization is filled with people who contain talent, in all kinds of combinations. If you take the time to identify what those combinations are, you will look at the people who work for you in a whole new way. You'll see the amazing resources they bring with them every day and long to use. That's why it's time to:

- Understand that the talent themes exist.
- Reject the old position that "anyone can be trained to do any job."

- Put an end to the attempt to fix "weaknesses."
- Function from a position based on employees' strengths.

By acknowledging that all your employees possess innate talents that can be emotionally engaged, you have taken the second step on The Gallup Path.

CHAPTER 3

The Route That Never Goes Astray

The Resource Waiting to Be Used

Like ancient roads that provided the means for trade, commerce, and wealth, employees can provide the pathway to profits and growth. So it makes excellent practical sense to pave the way for their talent to reach the world. With competition mounting on a global scale, no business, industry, or organization can afford to pay an employee for providing anything less than a great performance—which means one that is emotion driven.

Of course, there is a huge range within roles and situations, and among types of industry and organizations; diversity is a constant. Nonetheless, hundreds of performance-linked-to-outcome studies at Gallup, involving a highly diverse range of roles and positions, including those in sales, customer service, teaching, health provision, law enforcement, sports, and the arts, revealed fascinating information.

These analyses identify the exceptional contribution of talent, as opposed to other internal or external variables. It also measured the magnitude of the contribution on the employer.

We discovered that great organizations:

- Identify, select, and develop talent.
- Nurture their employees' strengths. Roles are constantly being adapted to better suit these strong points. Because true value comes from the best performers, the bar is continually raised. Outcomes are measured and compensation is tied to them.
- Train to develop individual strengths.
- Understand that knowledge can be transferred from one person to another, but is always specific to the situation.
- Bolster strengths so that profits will grow.

With this information in hand, the selection for the right talent to fit the right role can begin.

Talents and Profits: The Inseparable Duo

Our hundreds of studies proved time after time that talent makes a huge impact on profitable growth across every major type of occupation and industry. We also discovered that the effect of talent is reflected by how productive a person can become. The top 25 percent most productive individuals in all sorts of occupations were identified, reviewed, and studied in depth with regard to their performance and personal talents.

Ultimately, the results were clear: Only the best—consistently exemplified by the most productive—generated sustainable and real value. The key to highest individual performance lies in the unbeatable combination of experience, training, and talent. That's why it is imperative that the talent combinations of the best be compared with those of poor and average workers. Only then can their strengths be identified and channeled so that they, too, can spur growth.

It probably won't come as a big surprise to find out that

most employees fall into the average group. These people meet the basic criteria of what they do, and adhere to rules and policies that outline the boundaries of their jobs.

Poor performers fall into two groups. There are those unfortunate souls currently miscast in their roles. And there are new entrants, the "rough diamonds" with talent for the job for which they were hired, but who are in need of serious polishing in the form of training and experience.

But superior performers are something else. These rare people—rare because most talent is so underutilized—follow their instincts and thereby identify and develop their specialties. Almost always they do this on their own.

Interestingly, these superior performers focus on the outcome, not the steps. While they are not arrogant rule breakers, they emphasize results. Instinctively, they rely on their own talents, and their instincts pay off over and over again. For instance, individual studies determined that tapped-into talent accounts for an average gain of 40 percent in sales volume, with the top 10 percent of performers netting a whopping 80 percent of that amount. It also accounts for an average increase of 39 percent in teacher performance, 37 percent in the accomplishments of physicians, and an incredible 67 percent in the productivity of skilled and semi-skilled personnel alike.

When it comes down to the gulf between top performers and the rest, there are only two differences—but they are crucial:

1. No matter what occupation they are in or what role they play, top performers *always* define their work in terms of how much they can accomplish and how well they can do it. That, of course, will vary depending on the kind of industry or organization or business the person is in. Nevertheless, whether the end result is sales volume, reports finished, accounts balanced, arrests made, letters mailed, number of students going on to college, or lives saved, the

goal is the same: Measurable outcomes are the yardstick these people use. By doing so they link themselves to a visible effect. They put all their effort into seeing their goal realized. They want to see the difference they make.

2. Top performers tap into their natural talents and use them to perform their jobs extremely well. Although many of them find it difficult, if not impossible, to describe what exactly makes this happen, they are aware of one thing: Whatever the force is that is helping them, it is constant. It is the source that tells them the right decision to make, the right words to say, and the right way to get the job done the way it needs to be.

Talent influences business outcomes positively. Here are some examples of how sales growth is spurred when those emotion-driven talents are used to their utmost.

The Gift That Keeps on Giving

Even the biggest emotion doubters will come around when they see how talent affects their business. This is what happened to a curmudgeonly customer service manager of a large appliance manufacturer. While his view of customers was colored by years of dealing with every kind of complaint—"The perfect business world wouldn't allow any human interaction" was his skewed opinion—he eventually changed his mind.

For years his corporation had struggled to improve sales in a flat industry. Refrigerators, washing machines, and stoves are necessities, but they are also the kinds of products that move in a stable, highly predictable trend. Other than promotion, discounts, and rebates, there were few incentives to spark sales. But the manager had an idea.

He figured that if there was a range in the service performance of employees, and a range in the sales performance of dealers, then maybe there was a way to combine the best of both worlds. Top dealers offering superior service would increase sales volume.

First he tracked down the record of his best customer service employees and observed that they shared a pool of talents. They exhibited a gift for creating and maintaining steady relationships with others, who liked them in return. Additionally, they were dependable—and with sharp instincts, they could find solutions easily. He gave this group training in technical issues such as product inventory and logistics, and began his operation.

After several months he perceived that the most successful service representatives distinguished themselves by sharing some additional natural traits. Totally immersed in the needs of their clients, they were more competitive and displayed a take-charge attitude. These gifts, in combination, made the difference.

With this information in hand, the manager set up a telemarketing service to best serve his dealers. As a result of the manager's conversion to the talent philosophy, the top dealers exceeded their sales quota by 26 percent, outselling the average dealers, who were not included in the telemarketing operation, by more than $1 million each annually.

In another venue, the technological equivalent of bells and whistles wrapped in designs that rendered their computers near works of art gave a major manufacturer a boost—but soon after the new models were introduced, sales stalled. Still, a select few salespeople kept their numbers consistently high. This group was analyzed, and what they did extremely well—constant drive; thriving on measures and scores, which could then be compared to others; and an ability to naturally connect to their customers—was noticed. Thereafter, new employees were selected on the basis of similar talents, and their performance was monitored for the next twelve quarters.

After the initial four quarters, the employees hired for

these specific talents were putting out numbers slightly above those of the company's poor performers, about $846,000 per quarter. Another four quarters later, when training and experience were added to the talent combination, the talented group was not only producing 28 percent more sales than the poor segment, it leapt ahead of the sales volume tallied by the average salespeople by 22 percent. At the end of the twelve quarters the talented group rose above the rest, becoming the top performers. They netted a very substantial $2.9 million per quarter. Those at the very top netted more than $3.7 million per quarter.

One highly successful medical equipment manufacturer was another example. With each of the company's products worth several million dollars, the sales process, which took a while, tended to be complicated. So the selling talent pool was studied, developed, and perfected over more than a decade. In that period of time, the numbers of superior performers were augmented so that even the lowest-producing employee rose above what would have been average ten years ago. The special talent combinations of the members of this team contributed to the corporation's stunning tenfold increase in revenue—from $200 million to more than $2.5 billion.

In a related story, a huge provider of telecommunications chose and managed its telemarketing associates with one goal: Every one of them was expected to nail the sale. Sure, these people knew how to "speak." Certainly they were knowledgeable and employed the skills they learned. But something more than that was required to be above average. A really convincing pitch, it was discovered, required razor-sharp communication and the natural ability to connect emotionally and build trust with customers.

The telemarketers with talents in these areas were turned down less often (and hung up on a lot less frequently), completed more successful calls, and left their customers feeling satisfied. Considering how tough their calls were—often to people who didn't want to be bothered—their accomplishments were solid.

Then there was a renowned financial institution. If anything, this organization was top-heavy with knowledgeable advisers who could recite chapter and verse on stocks, bonds, mutual funds, and the variables they presented. After all, interpreting conflicting information in a mutable economy was part of their job description. But relaying information, no matter how in-depth it was or how many years the presenter had spent studying it, didn't translate into new customers.

When the institution examined the particular talents of top performers, multiple characteristics were detected. Strong organization and planning, impeccable follow-through on all commitments, a yearning to know more, the ability to take charge and make a stand about going in a certain direction, and the desire to have their performances measured and ranked against those of others in like positions were present. They were also able to sort through the best options to recommend what to choose.

Whereas their colleagues would see an incomplete puzzle, these gifted advisers saw pieces that did or did not fit together. Most important, they could determine the one or two investments that involved the least amount of risk along with more significant returns. These men and women were therefore able to offer something extra to their clients.

Investing money is always an intensely emotional issue because of the uncertainty involved. Big gains can be followed by staggering losses in a very short period of time. Being able to connect with a person who can act as guide through uncharted territory is extremely reassuring.

Knowledge and skills are important, but only talent holds the potential for top performance.

Other Work, Other Talents

Talent shines through in every profession when it takes the stage. The tour guide who has a "knack" for connecting with tourists does them and his theme park a huge service. By forging an emotional link with visitors, he makes them feel welcome and comfortable. They enjoy the experience (even when they might have been predisposed to hate it) and want to remember it. So they buy souvenirs and take lots of pictures. By the time they get home, they are already planning their next trip back. A single employee, whose talent fits his job perfectly, has created higher levels of net volume and sales just by being able to show who he is.

Data collected by Gallup point to the fact that wonderful teachers don't see themselves as mere information dispensers. Instead, they bring all of their own talents into the classroom and share them. One of the amazing assets of outstanding teachers is their knack to "see" each student as an individual with definite likes and dislikes who shows aptitude for certain subjects and weaknesses in others. But perhaps the biggest indicator of a life-changing teacher is the seemingly supernatural capacity to "read" their students' feelings and form deep relationships with them. A bond is forged that never breaks. It's no wonder that students with these kinds of experiences go on to succeed in higher education.

Law enforcement agents display an interesting array of talents as well. According to a study of exceptional performance in civilian protection, sheriffs in rural America demonstrate unique combinations of talent.

These officers of the law have deeply held beliefs about their mission. They focus on actions as they take them, and hold fast to the notion that they can do their jobs only when they are constantly vigilant.

In another study, the police officers in a relatively small city in the Midwest exhibit vigilance, assertiveness, and accommodation. The outstanding officers mix excellent communication and rapport with the ability to remain forceful; they can issue orders without getting angry. This helps them make cool decisions in dangerous situations. With a natural tendency to be alert and observant, they anticipate what will happen. Also, this remarkable group tolerates frustration extremely well and shrugs off criticism. They keep on working because their mission is always in the forefront of their minds. Finally, their accommodating natures help see them through all kinds of circumstances.

And then there are the finest officers in one of America's largest cities, who get their work done in the ever-present face of danger. They come to the job armed with special talent mixes: a natural predisposition to serve and a willingness to speak and act for those whom they feel need their help and protection.

In a city that has seen all kinds of crime numbers plummet, the police often credit recently forged links with communities as a major contributing factor. Establishing bonds with neighborhoods—that is, with people—created a different way for the police and civilians to interact with one another.

Firefighters show particular talents, too. If you have ever wondered why firefighters never hesitate before running into a burning building, here are the reasons. Data gathered in dozens of studies state that glory has little to do with it. Instead, two natural predispositions impel their behavior. One is the adrenaline surge that kicks in whenever they enter a burning building. Extraordinary firefighters, however, do it for another critical reason as well: their mission, which is to save lives.

Nurses, of course, save lives, too. Those on the front lines of a hospital can affect not only how efficiently the emergency room functions, but also how patients react when they arrive there. Scared, in pain, unsure of what is going to happen to them, people in need of medical assistance tend, understandably, to be tense and worried. Top nurses connect with the emotional trauma of their patients, understanding what these people are going through. Because of these nurses' unique talent combinations, patients respond both to them and the hospitals in which they work. In times of emotional upheaval, people remember who treated them well and paid attention to their pain. If they find themselves in need of medical assistance again, they will know where they will receive the care they need.

FOLLOW THE TALENT ROUTE

Are you convinced that talent is all around you, waiting to be tapped? The great organizations are; it's what helps them reach, and maintain, their rank. If you want your work group to excel, to be the best it can be, you must tap into the essence of what drives people to perform the very best they can, over and over again. You can count on it.

Evaluating that talent begins when the finest performers in each role are identified. Here's how the great organizations do it. They:

- Find out what makes top performers passionate about their work. It's the clue that leads to everything that follows.
- Pay a lot of attention to them to see how they build relationships.
- Keep track of their impact on others—great performers spur others to better work.
- Ask them how they process information as well as form their opinions about the work and the workplace.

By understanding that unique talent combinations lead to increased profits and growth, you have taken the third step on The Gallup Path.

CHAPTER 4

Steering toward Engagement

Engage the Present, Ensure the Future

For young Phil Esposito, awakening from a deep sleep and wresting himself from the warmth of his bed in the very early morning was worth the effort. Layering on sweaters to ward off the shocking predawn chill of the Ontario morning, Phil knew his father would already be up. Soon they would be driving on the dark, empty roads to the ice rink so that Phil could put in hockey practice time before school.

Phil loved playing hockey with the other boys—the speed it allowed him, the sound of his skates stroking the ice, the thrill of thwacking the puck into the net. It was great. His father was there with him, watching him improve while Phil enjoyed himself. Phil considered himself unbelievably lucky.

Then one morning something awful happened. In a fast move against an opponent, Phil's hockey stick cracked and broke. Shocked, he watched the lost half fly across the ice and hit the side of the rink. Skating over to pick it up, he realized that he had a huge problem on his inexperienced hands.

For one thing, he felt awful; he had disappointed his father sitting up in the stands, who expected better from him. Worse, he had blown the practice, future games, everything. He couldn't ask for another stick that he wanted so badly; money in his house was always tight. The pain of all that had suddenly transpired hit him like a hockey puck in the heart.

Dejected, he packed up his skates and headed outside to the car. When his father got in, he didn't say anything; he just dug into his pocket, counted out three dollars, and handed them to his son. "Why don't you buy a new hockey stick?" he asked.

Phil couldn't believe it. The stick, he knew, cost almost as much as his father earned in one day at the Algoma Steel Mill. Suddenly he realized that his father wasn't mad at him, or let down. In a moment of insight Phil realized that his father was doing everything in his power to make sure that his son pursued hockey. That's why his father made such an effort for him—he wanted him to do what he loved and win the games he played. A lot of people watching could enjoy the sport, too.

And that's exactly what happened. In 1971 he set the National Hockey League record for goals, an accomplishment that wasn't topped until 1982, when Wayne Gretzky surpassed his number. As a Boston Bruin, he was a team leader along with Bobby Orr. They helped their team win the Stanley Cup in 1970 and 1972. He also played for the Chicago Blackhawks and the New York Rangers.

Many years later, when Phil was inducted into the NHL Hall of Fame, he credited his father with setting him on the path to greatness. His father, able to see his raw strengths, had devoted his time to cultivate them, no matter what happened along the way.

In his Gallup interview, as part of a study on talent in best hockey teams, he recounted his father's influence.

Gallup: Tell me about the important events in your career.

My dad was a big supporter of mine. He would always come to the games. The first recollection I have is, I think, [was when I was] four years old. My dad was putting double runners on my feet, and he had built a rink in the backyard as my brother and I were playing hockey.

He made lots of sacrifices. You know that he came to every game we [my brother and I] played? But never said anything. The only thing he would say to us is this. When I got two goals I'd be waiting for him to say "way to go" and he'd say "you played pretty well, but you should have had three or four." He'd do it even when I was in the NHL. He did it until the day I retired. That night I said, "I should have had one" and he said, "You should have had more than one, my son, you should have had two or three for sure."

Gallup: Was anyone influential in your career?

I think Harry Sinden (coach) and Milt Schmidt (general manager) were careerwise very influential on me.

Gallup: Why?

Because they allowed me to play my own style. I don't know why coaches wouldn't understand that. The more I played my own style, the better I played.

The Medium That Grows Talent

Phil Esposito's recollection underscores an essential need of talent. In order for it to develop, another person who cares about the person displaying it must recognize it.

This truth plays out day after day, year after year, in all sorts of venues. Sports are a big one. Many athletes cite one or both parents as their champions from an early age. Those mothers and fathers didn't just attend games and cheer. Like Phil Esposito's father, they were aware that their son or daughter had something special, and they nurtured that gift so that it could grow. The same is true of scores of musicians, hotel housekeepers, dancers, convenience store attendants, singers, tellers, carpet installers, actors, and roofers. Often police and firefighters come from families long associated with those specific kinds of work, who understand and respect it. The same is true of chefs and numerous others. Then there are the great teachers who see the sparks talent gives off and steer students in the right direction.

In just about everyone's life, there is a cherished memory of trying and excelling rendered all the sweeter because someone who cheered you on was there to see it. Sometimes the person was a close relative or a friend. Whoever it was, though, you wanted to show them how good you could be.

That person spotted your talent before you did and helped you grow your gift into a strength. In that way you knew that someone important to you expected something important from you.

That person saw you perform at your best, which meant that you impacted others—or even one person—in your unique way. That significant relationship gave you the impetus to express who you were, and so make connections to others. (Think of how often Academy Award–winning actors thank their parents for sending them to acting classes, or a particular teacher who cultivated their talent. Without such people behind them, millions wouldn't be buying tickets to their films.)

Where work in great organizations is concerned, the same process takes place. Strengths are determined. The demands of a role are defined. The expectation of a person who is important to the employee is met.

At work that someone special who takes notice is the great manager. When this happens, something marvelous happens. Employees are *fully engaged* in their work because the immediate manager or supervisor makes it possible.

Engaged Employees, The Rare Resource

It may be obvious that within one company one unit is more productive than another. However, it probably isn't common knowledge that the variation in employee engagement *within* a company is greater than the variation of employee engagement *between* two companies in the same industry. Every organization we studied contained the best and worst examples of employee engagement within it.

To bring home just how the engagement of employees involves business unit levels, which are always overseen by a manager, consider the startling percentages of a Gallup study. Hundreds of diverse companies were studied that shared one extraordinary and troubling statistic. *In a majority of those companies only 20 to 30 percent of the employees were engaged in their work.* These companies were operating on a fraction of employee engagement. The most engaged work groups were the most productive. The rest tended to be average, mediocre, or downright destructive.

> Just because employees are abundant doesn't mean that they are engaged. They're not. Engaged employees are a rare and precious resource.

The Misguided Detour

Many organizations regard work as a necessary evil. They figure that employees are predisposed to dislike what they do. Not only that; they also manage from the perspective that when employees are at work, they want to be somewhere else. (Of course, when employees are not engaged in what they are doing this is usually true. While they are physically present, they are psychologically absent.)

This perspective ignores a consistent aspect of human behavior. "What do you do?" is often the first question people ask one another upon meeting for the first time. If they already know each other, the question is usually, "How's work?" Enormous value is placed on what a person does. For many people it is a leading indicator of self-worth, and its influence directly affects family, friends, the community in which each person lives, and society in general.

Unfortunately, numerous consultants and human resource associates have tried to define the "best workplace" by focusing only on what it is not and then assuming that the opposite dictates greatness.

Recently, Gallup conducted a study among Fortune 500 companies to learn about their efforts to change their culture for the better. We found that 80 percent of the organizations were doing some type of study; the most common was the "climate" or "employee attitude" survey. On average these analyses asked 150 questions and lasted for more than an hour. They tried to measure everything from opinions about a planned parking lot, to why employees were working for the company, to feelings about incentives concerning mostly pay and benefits. But the startling discovery was that 60 percent of the organizations studied reported being worse off after the surveys were taken than before. For one thing, the communication levels between employees and managers were seriously diminished. Second, the disconnect between senior management and employees was considered even wider.

The reason was simple. The studies were designed to view the organization from the top down. Unfortunately, the questions didn't address, much less solve, the real issues that employees were facing day in and day out at the local level. Nor did they include local accountability; these studies were never reported at the workplace level, so middle managers assumed that the issues would be resolved at the top. The middle managers felt that this information did not specifically address their local workplace conditions. And since they were not provided with practical guidelines to act upon, they felt no responsibility to react to them.

As one manager of a supermarket shrugged:

> It's as if they gave us the weather forecast for the entire country. But I live in Boulder; that's the report I need, because it will tell me what is going on and what to expect. Why should I pay attention to the big picture when it doesn't include what I need to see and respond to?

Next, the very purpose of the studies wasn't clear. Were they supposed to create an impression of how good morale was, or to identify pockets of dissent? The effort was rarely linked to the issue that really mattered: increasing the performance of the organization. Even worse, the studies attempted to replace dialogue. More than a few participants came away with the impression that their company was so out of touch with its employees that it was forced to ask dozens of questions just to find out who they were.

At Gallup we felt that looking at both the highest- and lowest-producing work groups was imperative in order to discover the conditions that consistently distinguish them. That's why we researched among all kinds of industries and organizations, identifying the issues that managers and employees alike can act upon.

We also felt that the ultimate goal would be to identify the cultural conditions that attracted and nurtured top talent as well as those that drove negative attitudes and defeating behavior.

As a result of this mammoth effort, a group of twelve highly focused questions known as the Q^{12}* were posed to employees within the aforementioned hundreds of companies.

The results are in. Great managers run productive work-places whenever these twelve conditions are met.

THE CULTURAL BYPASS

One more myth must bite the dust: At its core, corporate culture is never—*never*—an organizational phenomenon, the kind that has been played up by dozens of CEOs. In reality the culture of an organization is a multifaceted entity, with as many identities and variations as there are managers and work groups. That's right: Each manager and each work group has its own culture.

Think of it this way: Lincoln Center for the Performing Arts in New York City is an organization that houses opera, ballet, modern dance, musical theater, symphony orchestras, solo artists in concert—the list goes on. Each one is a cultural entity unto itself, with very specialized work groups managed by very different kinds of people. Each unit has separate standards for employees, because each person has special talents. Ultimately, however, each unit has the same goal: to perform as brilliantly as possible to affect as many audiences as possible, touch them emotionally, and convince them to return for more performances.

So attempting to dictate one culture per organization is a waste of time. But it is important to remember that within each work group, the culture is the glue that keeps it together, creating so integrated a machine that each person's efforts perfectly dovetail with another's. In great organizations, enhanced synchronicity is the secret to achieving greater results while using existing resources. It not a matter of working harder—just smarter. That's why what really counts as culture is shaped by the Q^{12}.

Attention Really Must Be Paid

The largest study Gallup ever conducted on the attitudes and behaviors of outstanding employees and teams reached two central conclusions. The first identified the set of twelve conditions that impact the outcome of every level of business. The second proved that the responsibility for and success of these conditions lies with the manager and each employee within the manager's work group.

These extraordinary findings turn upside down the whole concept of how an organization should be run. That's because the twelve conditions are based squarely on what employees value.

Traditionally, organizations undervalue how employees feel about their work, workplace, customers—in fact, just about everything that affects the job they do. Instead, productivity, cutting costs, profitability, and growth are the issues that get the most attention. In stark contrast, the Q^{12} proves a principal driver of productivity, cost production, safety, low turnover and—guess what?—profitability and growth.

Even more intriguing, unlike most measures, which describe the recent-past performance of an organization, the Q^{12} explains current performance in relation to the future health of key financial outcomes.

Additionally, great organizations realize that what is good for a person also benefits the organization. Instead of the old method of trying to fit a person to a job, there is a new and very simple model: When individuals work at jobs that are meaningful to them, they simultaneously meet the core business objectives of the organization that hired them. This cause-and-effect link holds true across all types of organizations. Size and function make no difference. Basically, the Q^{12} is a global system that employs a single language everyone can speak.

Even better, the effects of the Q^{12} are enduring and sustainable—unlike the short-lived attempts to "motivate" and "raise the morale" of employees.

Most important, the Q^{12} unleashes the full engagement potential of individuals. It stands in complete contrast to the way organizations typically pigeonhole employee engagement as something that only comes from earning more money and being goaded with incentives. Instead, it shows that full engagement is a product not only of the way employees think but also of how they feel. And the way people feel is all about emotions.

Now that you have a new insight into the special strengths of individuals, it's time to apply them so that your employees can make an even stronger contribution to their roles, their teams, and their workplace environment. Each and every one of these talents influences the Q^{12}, the twelve conditions of a great workplace.

Twelve Courses to Follow

The Q^{12} define the conditions of a great workplace.

1. I know what is expected of me at work.
Without expectations, it is impossible to assess progress. Many managers do, of course, set and define goals; they trip up, however, because they overoperationalize the jobs. By putting all the focus on describing steps to follow, they create an environment that communicates a robotized message. Employees hear a company line that states, "Check your mind at the door; do your job this way and you will meet expectations."

This kind of one-size-fits-all approach completely ignores the fact that individuals approach work with their special styles. Even worse, some managers think that role expectations are contained in a job description—but they often miss the fine details.

When I was hired at a well-known law firm to work in the executive dining room, the job description was a perfect fit: two years' experience as a waitperson, pleasant manner, must wear specific uniform—the basics. I had worked at a lot of restaurants over the last few years: diners, cafés, coffee shops, all busy with a lot of turnover. I was told that I'd have a lot of people to serve—no problem there—but I wasn't totally filled in on what to expect. My "people skills" were regarded as intrusive, and I was expected to read people's minds and anticipate what they wanted before they asked for it. Sure, after a while I might be able to do that, but not right away. Also, after I was hired I was told that I'd have to pass around hors d'oeuvres at cocktail parties, which I didn't feel comfortable doing. Basically, I was expected to keep quiet and do my job. But I couldn't do "my" job the way I like to do to it: talking about what was on the menu, the chef's mood, the weather, which always made me suggest certain dishes. I wish the manager had been up front with me from the start, so that I could have made an informed decision.

2. I have the materials and equipment I need to do my work right.

More than anything else, information is the top necessity for every employee. While lacking the necessary tools can turn the desire to complete a job into an exercise in frustration, not having the most up-to-date information will prevent the completion of a job. In less effective work groups, the manager controls all resources and information as a way to protect his power and authority. Great workplaces are different, not because everyone gets anything they ask for but because of the openness, the clear two-way flow of communication about the resources needed to do the job right and the resources that are available.

I was given what everyone else had—a desk and a chair, a computer and keyboard, and a phone—when I was hired as an assistant to the public relations director of an electronics company. Then I was given a whole lot more: a file of the past year's press releases so that I could see how they were written and what kinds of messages they were giving. I sat in on meetings where I could observe how the future was being planned out. I received the same e-mail as the director, so I had up-to-date information every day. Because of this I could answer questions quickly and correctly. Also, it made me feel that my job, and therefore how I did it, was important.

3. At work, I have the opportunity to do what I do best every day.

No matter what the official company line is, or the expectations of a role, or the regulations of an organization, people will end up doing what they do best. But if they aren't doing it in the right job, their best gets lost. In great organizations, the most productive work flows when a person's innate gifts are matched to a role that celebrates them. Gallup research indicates that an individual's talents are strong, recurring, and unchanging patterns relating to how each person filters input and responds to it. Talent is not a lightbulb; it can't be turned on or off at will.

I was hired as an office manager for a travel agency because of my organizational skills. But I loved talking to the agents about the trips they were arranging, and I started telling them about where I had gone and what I'd seen and experienced. If I hadn't traveled to a place I wanted to go, I read up on it as much as I could and visited Web sites. One of the senior agents asked me if I would take calls as an intermediary—that is, talk to customers about where they were thinking of going and give them feedback and suggestions. Eventually a new job was created for me, where I spoke to local groups about the agency and what it had to offer, told through my own experiences. This is the best job I've ever had.

4. In the last seven days, I have received recognition or praise for doing good work.
Singling out excellent work and praising it goes a long way toward recognizing the individual contributions of employees. Not surprisingly, it adds to their sense of accomplishment. Recognition should be tied to the desired outcome and talents directed that way. When an employee receives recognition, she sees herself progressing in her role, thus seeing her value grow.

> I work for a national accounting firm with many offices in many cities. I like what I do but I always thought of myself as the third accountant from the left. But about a year ago a new manager came into our office and made some interesting changes. For me, the most compelling one was his singling out work for praise. I know he didn't do it indiscriminately, as if it was the "right" thing to do. What he did was make it a point to notice that really complicated return, and then call the person in who worked on it and let him or her know how impressed he was with the work. The first time he called me in I thought I had done something wrong, and he anticipated that. Immediately, he told me that he wanted to thank me for a job very well done. I felt great; not only was I getting better at what I was doing, I was recognized for it. It's one thing when people don't complain about your work; that way you just assume that you're doing okay. But when it's singled out, you begin to understand that you bring value to the company you're working for. There's nothing like that personal notice.

5. My supervisor, or someone at work, seems to care about me as a person.

Employees don't leave companies. They leave managers and supervisors whom they feel don't care about them either as individuals or as employees. So it's not surprising that when asked if they want to be managed, most employees answer with a resounding "no." But if an employee has enjoyed just one good managerial experience, welcoming management once again is a given. Caring makes the difference.

Said a twenty-year veteran of ad agencies whose artwork has been seen by millions:

> I've toiled under managers from hell; there's no other way I'd put it. I quit one big-paying job because the man I worked "under" crossed a big line. My father, who lived in another city, suffered a massive heart attack and I dropped everything to fly out to be with him and my mother and sister. The manager kept calling, wanting to know when I'd be back. And then he overnighted work to me—in the hospital! That was it. I sent the work back with "I quit" scrawled across it. When I looked for another job, I was skittish about a new boss. I was about a year into the next job, which I was really enjoying, when my mother became seriously ill. "Uh-oh," I thought; "here we go again." But I was wrong. This time, as soon as I told the manager, he told me to get on the first plane out and charge it to the company. He told me not to worry and to do what I needed to; my job would be waiting when I got back. That was five years ago. I never thought I could stand "management" again, but he redefined it for me.

6. There is someone at work who encourages my development.

Most people want to achieve more proficiency in what they do; it's human nature to want to improve, to overcome challenges, and to come out on top. Unfortunately, most organizations hold fast to policies that do anything but promote growth and development. That's because instead of fostering expansion of an employee's abilities, they focus on weaknesses. Those "soft spots," they think, require attention. All this does is emphasize what a person is not, rather than celebrate what a person is. Demoralizing and counterproductive, this is the way that many organizations try to force their personnel to change.

Change can be an effective means to improvement, particularly when it involves learning a new skill. But once again, it can backfire quickly if the training fails to enhance a person's hardwiring.

For the past forty years another factor has been filed in the growth folder. That factor is promotion. And while it is the rare individual who turns down a promotion, with its reward of increased income, benefits, and title, most employees are not comfortable with a new position that ignores their strengths.

After eight years as a drug representative I figured that no one would ever ask me about what makes me "tick." So I was flabbergasted when a new manager asked to meet with me, at my convenience, to talk about my development, as well as how I could invest what I have in order to make the company more profitable. After my years in this job I do have ideas about what I can to better advantage, but until now no one wanted to listen. Basically I had been told to "do it this way. This is what works. If your numbers grow eventually you'll get a promotion." Getting a promotion isn't the most important thing for me. It's about improving and being rewarded for it. But now I feel like I can develop in my job in my own way. What a relief.

7. At work my opinions seem to count.

Innovative ideas are priceless. Every organization searches for them; they bring a real competitive edge. But often companies overlook the suggestions of their employees. Great organizations know this is a costly mistake. When ideas—from every person—are encouraged, the viable ones can be processed and implemented. Understandably, contributions like these make employees feel valued; when that happens they are glad to offer more ideas, because they know they are actively improving the company they work for.

Said a relatively new employee of an ice cream manufacturer:

> I had what I thought was a really terrific idea: ask customers what kinds of ice cream they'd like, that they never had before. Since we don't have retail outlets, I thought that running a contest would be fun, and the reward would be a free year's supply. I told my supervisor, who brought me into a marketing meeting to pitch the idea. I was nervous, but I also thought, "This is great; I'm being taken seriously." Everyone listened—and they actually did what I suggested. Now a lot more of the people I work with are piping up with their ideas. No one is afraid that they'll look stupid or their ideas won't be considered. Even when the answer is no—and of course sometimes it is—the reasons are always explained, not shot down.

8. The mission or purpose of my company makes me feel my job is important.

Being part of the bigger picture is a very compelling notion. It comes under the heading of *emotional compensation*, because it can't be bought and paid for; instead, it is perceived. Stretching themselves to make a difference comes naturally when employees see that what they do has a profound impact. In return, they tend to honor their commitment to their employer. When this happens, the company represents the values of its workers; everyone, from bottom to top, shares the same goals. Obviously, it is much more rewarding to feel joined to the same mission, which will impact the outside world in some way, than it is to simply complete a task.

That's why, in most organizations, the highly popular "mission" statement often fails miserably. How could it not? Every person has a singular sense of purpose, finding different meanings in similar situations. A one-size-fits-all mission can't mean the same thing to every person. In the end individuals must know if the company looks at the world the same way they do. That's the way they determine whether their own purpose meshes with that of their company.

A salesman at a store that sells home supplies explained:

> I've been told, more than once, that my view of the world is naive at best. I want to believe that a company can make a difference in the world, and really improve life for lots of people.
>
> I've worked in a lot of places over the years, everything from mom-and-pop shops to conglomerates. I never felt totally comfortable in any of them because I couldn't buy into their "purpose." I don't have a problem with making money—I'm not that naive—but I don't expect that I'll agree with what a company does just because it pays me. Where I'm working now I see how what I'm doing helps people because the store shows it to me. It shares letters and e-mails from customers, who write about how we helped them to improve their homes, make them more comfortable and attractive. That gives me a real feeling of satisfaction. Everyone should be able to go home to a place where they feel good.

9. My associates or fellow employees are committed to doing quality work.

Not surprisingly, when employees are asked if *they* are committed to quality, they answer in the affirmative. After all, who would want to turn out inferior work? But when asked about the commitment to quality by their associates, the answer expands. Employees want their colleagues to share their dedication. This goes to the very center of why emotions must be recognized. It is impossible to assign a person to a team and expect him to accept whatever is being said. He will really join the team, however, thus becoming an active member of it, when he perceives that doing so will leverage him and his group to excellence. Identification with a shared commitment is crucial for the work group to turn out a quality product or service.

In instances like these, problems can bring out a stronger team spirit. Employees sworn to deliver quality work regard problems as a way to bind their team. The team power not only overcomes the crisis; it goes on to correct whatever process they use in order to avoid future problems. It makes sense, therefore, that employees want to be part of an organization that enables them to excel.

The chief of security for a large hotel usually filled with conventions and other events told us:

> I view my job as part of the security team in the hotel as incredibly important, now more than ever. Teamwork is especially essential to what we do. We must trust each other, and be able to rely on one another all the time. There has to be a strong connection among us because we have to know that we'll back each other up no matter what happens. Every one of the men and women on the security force here feels that way. I couldn't dictate it to them; they had to believe that what they are doing counted, otherwise they wouldn't be able to do it. I know that from experience. That's why I give everyone

who wants to join our team a probation period to see who they are and how they feel. It's the only way I can be sure whether someone will fit or not, which means whether he or she will perform to the best of his or her ability.

10. I have a best friend at work.
Often organizations do not encourage the notion of friends at work, much less "best" friends. These chummy people, it is believed, may be goofing off, spending too much chatting, laughing at private jokes. What possible good could they be doing for the company?

Actually, quite a lot. Impressive numbers bear this out: Having a best friend at work improves a person's chances of being engaged by an amazing 54 percent. Not having one, on the other hand, reduces chances to zero. Employees who report having a best friend at work are more likely to report that:

- They received praise or recognition for their work in the previous week (43 percent higher than the average).
- Someone at work encouraged their development (37 percent higher than the average).
- They have a co-worker committed to quality (35 percent higher than the average).
- In the prior six months someone at work talked to them about their progress (28 percent higher than the average).
- The mission of their company makes them feel that their job counts (27 percent higher than the average).
- Their opinions count (27 percent higher than the average).
- They have the opportunity to do what they do best every day (21 percent higher than the average).

Amazingly, using the word "best" to describe a work friend is a defining characteristic of great work groups. Each person acknowledges that co-workers will help out during times of duress. It's an enormous trust builder.

But it's obvious that having a best friend doesn't mean that two people exclude others. On the contrary, the emotional, supportive bond, which supplies a meaningful two-way relationship, makes quite a positive impression on other members of the work group, too. People who report having a best friend at work manage stress a lot better because they know they can express it within their group and not be penalized or ostracized for doing so.

Today this is more important than ever. In an age of rapid change, reorganization, and mergers and acquisitions, having a best friend at work may be the real way to achieve effective change integration and adaptation. That's because deep friendships are valued and respected as a means for learning, getting useful feedback on assignments, evaluating progress, and all-important emotional bonding.

A fashion editor remembered:

Joan, who was the advertising director, and I met in the conference room about two weeks after we started working at the same magazine. I admired her bracelet, and we were off and running. We discovered that we had a lot in common, and that gave us a connection separate from work. Whenever either of us lived through a tough day at work, we could let off steam in each other's office. We laughed a lot—and we got a lot done, too, with ideas flying at a nonstop pace. Over the next several years we both went through personal crises, and one of the things that made them tolerable was that we could count on each other. Then she received a huge offer at a different magazine in another city. It was just too good to refuse and she took it. I stayed where I was for a while but it was never the same again and eventually I left, too.

11. In the last six months, someone at work has talked to me about my progress.

What employees are doing well should be brought to their attention. Reviewing these "winning plays" every six months gives employees a clear awareness of their strengths so that they can keep building on them. Getting this kind of regular feedback is a terrific incentive to keep on improving.

A cashier in a department store related:

> I was amazed at my first six-month review because I thought it would be the usual kind of time waster: You do "this" okay but . . . "that" didn't happen.
>
> It turned out that one of the salespeople on my floor observed something I like to do, which is saying something about their purchase to each customer. It's always true, like "this is beautiful" or "that's such a pretty color." Almost every day the customer says something in return, and we have a mini conversation. Well, that salesperson noticed that those customers usually didn't head for the door. Instead, they would browse some more, and buy something else. The salesperson told the floor manager, who told me this at the review. I couldn't believe that (a) someone took notice of me and reported something good about me, and (b) I was being praised for something I do naturally. As much as I liked my job before, I enjoy it a whole lot more now.

12. This last year, I have had opportunities to learn and grow at work.

After a year, it's time for an employee to answer this question: "Am I better or worse at what I do?" That means answering a bigger question, which is: "What have I learned that I can apply to my performance to make it better?"

Learning must be targeted to enhance existing strengths; otherwise it won't add to an employee's personal and professional growth. When it is aimed properly, employees respond with a highly emotional reaction: engagement.

In today's ever-changing work environment, productivity stems from working smarter. This is why work environments of superior organizations promote and reinforce strength-focused learning. Where learning is constant and supported, innovation follows. So does the realization that the human mind is ever capable of discovering new ways to new places, where new customers await.

An administrative assistant in the billing office of a real estate firm told us:

> I'd say the best thing that happened to me in the last year—the fourth year I've worked here—is that I learned as much in that time as I did in the first year I was here. I like to learn, but now I see how that knowledge can be applied to make my work easier and more effective and less time consuming. I feel that each year I'm progressing, advancing to the next level, and that the people I work with meet me halfway. I can't imagine ever leaving here: It's the first place I've ever worked where I feel that I'm actually growing in the job.

Don't Deviate from the Designated Route

Great managers follow the sequence of the Q^{12} to the letter for a good reason: The conditions are like a bridge that spans from a company outward.

The foundation is laid with conditions one and two. Like colossal blocks, they address the primary concerns of the employee—namely, what the job is going to entail and having the proper tools to get right to it.

The struts are put in with conditions three, four, five, and six. Now talent must fit and be recognized, or the bridge will prove unstable. Knowing that the bridge will receive the care it needs will be acknowledged, and the structure will begin to take shape.

Conditions seven, eight, nine, and ten represent the suspension wires, which connect with one another; each one is important but cannot do the job by itself. Teamwork must exist in order for the bridge to be ready to function at its maximum capacity.

Finally, the bridge is ready to do its best, as reflected in conditions eleven and twelve. Information will travel back and forth across the bridge, allowing products and services to flow to customers. In times of stress the bridge will sway but not fall, because all of its parts are tightly engaged. As time goes on it will become stronger, because it will be viewed as resilient and majestic.

This new bridge, providing a strong, reliable structure that both can rely on, will join those two separate entities: organizations and customers.

ENGAGED EMPLOYEES FEEL GOOD ABOUT THEIR JOBS AND THEMSELVES

If you want a productive, positive team, following the Q^{12} is the route for you. Forget about the old management rules that begin with, "Here's what *I* want." Change directions to ask employees, "What do *you* want?" This is the way toward employee engagement, one of the most important milestones on The Gallup Path. Putting the Q^{12} to work for you is the map that leads right to it.

Great organizations do the following:

• They follow the Q^{12}, because they know it impacts on the way employees view their workplace and themselves on an emotional level. It is this level that leads to engagement.

- They acknowledge that the success of the Q^{12} is the manager's responsibility because it concerns each employee within a work group.
- They sum up the way employees emotionally respond to the Q^{12} this way:

"Focus me."

"Equip me."

"Know me."

"Help me see my value."

"Care about me."

"Help me grow."

"Hear me."

"Help me see my importance."

"Help me feel proud."

"Help me build mutual trust."

"Help me review my contributions."

"Challenge me."

By realizing the power of the Q^{12} and accepting what it can do for your organization, you have taken the fourth step on The Gallup Path.

CHAPTER 5

Directions for Enhancing and Managing Employee Engagement

The Link Forgers

Ask Peter, a senior executive at a glass manufacturing firm, what the role of a manager is, and he'll roll his eyes in response. With some degree of disdain, he says:

> All I know is that everyone wants to be a manager. The problem is, most people don't have a clue how to "manage" people. Too many of them think it's about a better salary, a bigger office, a grander title—and the chance to boss people around. We've got to stop making becoming a manager a reward. Instead we've got to start rewarding great managers. Frankly, I've seen promotions to managerial positions hurt both the person moved up—because he or she doesn't know what to do, and now that person doesn't do that work that got them the promotion in the first place—and the people who report to the manager. Honestly, do we really need managers anyway?

Peter has a point. In many organizations the manager's role is not as important as it used to be—and may in fact be an obstacle to speed, agility, and flexibility. If employees are supposed to be self-motivated, self-reliant, and self-directed individuals, working efficiently in their teams, why would anybody need a manager? No organization can afford to pay an army of managers just to sign papers, authorize procedures, and check on other people.

This perspective, however, avoids a vitally important viewpoint of great organizations: Managers' chief responsibility lies in helping employees on their team unleash their human potential. No system, process, or self-directed team—irrespective of how modern, fashionable, or flawless it may be—can ever take the place of a great manager. That's because great managers act as the emotional connection between employees within work groups, between employees and customers, and between employees and the organizations they work for. In effect, they act as the emotional engineers who set the reactions in place and watch them take effect.

Reaching all employees, and helping them utilize their distinct talent is the most vital activity there is within an organization—and it can only be executed well one employee at a time. In great organizations, that's what managers do.

Engaged employees are immersed in jobs that utilize their natural strengths every day. It's not much of a stretch to think of employee engagement as the optimal functioning of a car. When an employee is fully engaged, the car is in the right gear to drive to maximal productivity and efficiency.

Measurement of the twelve conditions of highly productive workplaces—the Q^{12}—gives specific feedback about the areas in which the gear differential is off.

When gears don't synchronize with one another to accomplish optimal output, it's the job of a great manager to fix them. At the same time, when the gears work perfectly, it's up to the manager to pay attention to them so that they stay that way, which will help them perform for years to come.

In the great speedway of business, the manager determines the best cars for different types of races, helps them run at top efficiency, and then—most important—steps back to watch them succeed.

Great managers want each employee to feel a certain amount of tension. Defining the right outcomes creates that tension and the thrill and pressure of being out there by one-self, with a very definite target.

That's why great managers employ a variety of innovative methods to deal with particular situations. They always find a way to rank, rate, or count as many of the desired outcomes as possible. If this becomes difficult, they sit down with the employees and ask them how *they* would like to be assessed, because they want the members of their team to "own" the measures. They also don't give in to the first objection that so many managers hear—that is, "You can't measure my job." If very complex roles like that of the president of the United States can be evaluated, so can a person's role in a team. If a role really cannot be measured, it is a non-job.

Great managers exist in every company, all over the world. But the problem is that, on average, only one of every ten managers (and only two in every ten employees) unleashes human potential intuitively. Consistently setting human nature free to be as wonderful as it can be is the standard of great organizations.

Superior managers do this by turning "ordinary" employees into engaged performers. They identify and understand the employees in the work group, but their most important function is to turn on the emotional "switch" that sends the talent current to light up the right role. That's why the manager doesn't ever lose sight of the demands of a role, the strengths of the individual, and the desired outcome of the job.

The Four Keys of Great Managers

Great managers employ just four keys to meet their goals:

1. When selecting someone, they opt for talent, not simply experience, intelligence, or determination.
2. When setting expectations, they understand the importance of defining the right outcomes, not the steps to get there.
3. When motivating someone, they focus on the person's strengths, not their weaknesses.
4. When developing someone, they help find the right fit between talent and role. And they use the Q^{12} as a guide to understanding and developing their employees.

Managing the Q^{12}

Every great manager knows where each employee stands in each of these twelve conditions. While focusing on four primary keys to unleash and maximize a person's performance, great managers almost instinctively build the twelve conditions into their work environment. They know that only in the best environment can they get their employees' talents to blossom.

1. Define the right outcomes.
At the basis of the engagement process are the basic expectations of a role. These come down to two issues: "Do I know what the desired outcomes of my role are for today?" and "Do I know if the desired outcomes of my job have been accomplished today?"

Often, managers get fixated on defining the "right" steps of the job rather than how to guide very different people with very diverse styles toward a productive outcome. The best managers tell us they define the right outcomes first, and then let each employee find a personal route toward those outcomes. This approach allows for true growth via all individuals' discovery of their own "path of least resistance." It appreciates and values differences between employee styles and flow, and truly encourages individuals to use their talents to the fullest possible extent. This approach also encourages employees to take responsibility.

One great manager describes it this way:

> I used to work at an entertainment conglomerate where job descriptions were practically etched in stone. It was like placing an ad for a car and requesting that it come equipped with four wheels. Okay, every car has four wheels, so the understanding is that it will roll. But what about speed, safety features, power, fuel efficiency, and design, much less performance? Job descriptions are activity lists with no connection to business outcomes. They contain rules on how to perform those activities, but they fail miserably on capitalizing on individual strengths. And there is no distinction in a job description between superior, poor, or average performance. You know what they are? A default design that leads organizations to expect mediocre results. What I've seen over and over again is that superior performance is always more about what is absent in a job description than what is actually in it.

2. Provide the necessary tools.

If the matching of skills with tools is not thoroughly examined, there can be great cost for either the individual, the organization, or both. For example, many organizations have come into the computer era boldly and rapidly. Salespeople have been supplied with laptop computers to enable them to better manage time, keep accounts organized, communicate with the home office, and so on. Often, however, the skills and knowledge of, or even interest in, using this tool are not there.

This is often viewed as a training problem, so the salespeople are sent off to classes to build up their comfort level with computers. In a few cases the salespeople respond and feel more at ease with their computers, but the rest learn the basics and play solitaire or spend time surfing the Net. This reaction undermines the organization's return on this substantial investment.

One company dealt with this problem in an unusual way. The manager, a man in his fifties, called a meeting and confessed that he was a computerphobe:

I know we're all supposed to love them, but I don't. I don't care for all the paraphernalia, like Palm Pilots, either. But the reality is, we all have to use them. So here's what I'd like to do. This year, I want to do a "Bring your son or daughter to work day to show you how to use your computer." If anyone feels skittish about this, believe me: My daughter, who is eleven, knows she is far beyond me in computer skills. She would love to teach me. And you know what? I've gotten to the point where I realize she can do it. It also gives us something to share and to talk about at home.

Sometimes the definition of "tools" gets stretched. On one level, an operational problem like needing a new chair can be easily measured. On another level, in today's non-hierarchical, flatter organization, where communication travels among all employees and status is defined by salary and performance rather than position on a corporate ladder, the old measures of prestige, like titles, mean less than they ever did. That's why employees seek clues that define where they stand in the social order of things. Materials and "stuff" have become those indicators. So a manager may receive a request to put a conference table in an employee's office, only to discover the main reason given is "because Julie has one in her office, and I am just as important as she is." There is a relational component to this condition as well. With fewer prestige markers, testing one's relationship with a manager becomes very important. It comes down to this: "How does the manager *feel* about me and about what I am doing? How much recognition am I getting from her?"

Knowing this, the best managers shift decisions to the employee. Managers provide criteria for employees to use in making decisions, such as: "How is this new tool or piece of equipment going to help (a) you as an employee, (b) our company, and (c) our customers?" This broadens the employee perspective, expands clarification on desired outcomes, and builds better communication between individuals and managers. It also takes the manager out of the traditional "parent" role and allows for true ownership and accountability.

One manager recalled:

I knew that Carla wanted to be noticed when she demanded a better office. A lot of people were being moved around because of renovations, and she told me she deserved an office with more windows because she placed more people in jobs in the last year than anyone else in our employment agency. I knew she already made more money than the other agents did, but this request came as a surprise. Carla was not the demanding type. Finally she told me that her success wasn't being recognized by the company in a way that everyone else could see; she wanted others to know that she earned something that was visible, and the only way to do that was to go through me. When I asked her how getting the bigger office would help her perform, she was stumped. "I suppose sitting in a bigger office looks good to interviewees, but, to be honest, it really doesn't make a difference in the jobs they're placed in," she told me. "A nicer office would be an ego boost for me, but now I see that it won't add to revenue. But you know what would help? A more comfortable chair, so that I don't squirm in my seat when I'm talking to clients." I agreed, and Carla picked out the chair that suited her best.

3. Select for talent.

The best managers clearly see the specific talents needed for every role. Proven managers rebuff the misguided, short-sighted belief that "some roles are so easy, they don't require any talent." Great managers consistently tell us that their best performers—in any role—reveal specific recurring patterns of thought, feeling, and behavior. The most efficient front-desk clerks in hotels, for example, have a talent for establishing trust with patrons within the first seven seconds of an interaction. Exceptional telephone service and sales personnel possess a "third ear" or the ability to connect visually and emotionally with people they talk to, either on the phone or in person. Outstanding accountants see patterns in numbers and "hear" the message or story they tell.

Great managers think that excellence should be revered in every job. They see their task as defining the talents needed for every role, and then choosing the appropriately talented person for that role. This way, the person does what he or she does best every day.

Each manager may have a different method of doing it, but they almost invariably start with a profile of each employee's strengths and obtain a qualified feedback on his most predominant talents. Then they follow up with one-on-one interactions with each person to develop a common understanding of his talent, current level of knowledge, and skills. And they keep the dialogue open. Great managers know that the focus is on creating strong connections with each of their individual employees.

During the course of their conversation the manager may ask about the kinds of activities that the person is naturally drawn to; the activities where rapid learning happens and satisfaction kicks in. The details that interest him most about his job, along with the specific things that make him passionate, are also covered. The understanding is that employees who say "no" to any of the twelve conditions—which means that the condition is not fulfilled—may not feel that they already possess the skills or knowledge they need. But they may also say it because they do not feel that the role really lets them use their natural talent.

These are the questions that great managers ask themselves most frequently:

- Are roles defined properly? If not, adjust the job to customize the fit with the employee's natural talent. Great managers try to go from the players to the plays, rather than squeezing everyone into the same standard role.
- Are there too many policies and procedures attached to the role? Top managers try to redefine the roles around the *outcomes* desired and avoid the "standard way of doing things."
- Does a role need to be clarified? Superior managers symbolically hold up a mirror in front of employees and provide continuous feedback on performance and team impact. Paradoxically, natural strengths are often invisible to the holder; it is through the relationship with the manager that an employee can gain confidence.
- Is this job being valued enough? Is this the kind of role everyone wants to abandon, because employees feel that the company does not attach any real value to it? If this is the case, great managers measure everyone's performance and bring attention to every role. They make sure that excellence in every role is valued.

Said a supervisor at an investment house:

When Jake was hired as the newest of a long line of mail room workers, he was organized, reliable, and cheerful, but soon he got the drift that his job wasn't regarded as important. A lot of people didn't acknowledge him when he came around; "thank you" was something he heard only once in a while. So it wasn't that surprising when he started to slack off, not delivering mail when it was due and not bringing up the messenger packages as soon as they came in. I knew I couldn't defend the poor behavior of a lot of employees, but I could, I thought, change the way Jake regarded his job.

One day I walked with him as he made deliveries, and explained what was going to whom and why. I told him about what the sealed envelopes contained: financial information about clients that we trusted him with. I told him that a lot of people wouldn't do his job well because they could lose papers and misplace packages. Everyone needed Jake to do his work well—even if they were too narrow-sighted to see it.

Jake didn't say anything to me at the time, but he improved his performance from then on. One day he handed me a sealed note on his rounds. It read: "You're right. Thanks for seeing that what I do counts, too. Jake."

4. Focus on each person's strengths.

Obviously, recognition can be either positive or negative. In their wisdom, great managers do not treat them as opposites. Instead, they think that the opposite of any kind of recognition is just being ignored. Effective recognition, in their eyes, holds the following characteristics: It is positive in nature, immediate, and real-time to performance. Additionally, it is specific about what is being praised, and close to the action and done in a way that best impacts the recipient. Many organizations have formal recognition programs of limited effectiveness. This is probably because these programs do not always give employees a clear idea of what, exactly, is being recognized—profit, growth, and so on.

Positive recognition is often thought of as coming strictly from supervisors or managers, but in Gallup's study of outstanding managers, we found that employees cherish praise and recognition from peers and customers as well. Co-workers know intimately the particulars of a job, and when they notice and commend excellence, it is interpreted as a special event.

How often should people be praised? As a general rule, about once a week. Frequent praise is so important because whenever someone does something, there are consequences. Those outcomes will affect whether the employee will engage in that behavior again.

What is the best way to give praise? Great managers know that admiration is a universal requirement—but also that some rules apply. Compliments must be tied to outcomes; they can be given to the same person several times in the course of a week. Also, it must be individualized, predictable, genuine, and given only when it is deserved. On the other hand, giving praise when it isn't warranted does not serve anyone's purpose.

Recognition took on a whole new meaning to me when I first became a sales manager of half a dozen very seasoned salespeople. Our high-tech organization has always been clear about the value that great salespeople bring to the table. But when I first started in my new role, I was blown away with the talent and technical competence that they all displayed as well as the relationships they had forged. At the beginning I traveled with the reps and called on their customers and potential clients with them. After each call we would discuss it and, being a positive person (maybe to a fault), I would always highlight the strengths of each person and how they handled this and that. But the tables got turned on me. After the calls, the reps began to give me feedback on what I had done or offered that they had found particularly helpful. I really didn't know how to take this. But their recognition of me actually established clearly in my mind what my role should and can be in bringing value to them and their customers, not just the other way around. What my value is to them was never covered in any of the management training I went through. It was all about maximizing their value to the organization. It was through their immediate, real-time recognition of me that clarified my role. It was a very powerful lesson that I will never forget.

5. Caring counts.

A productive workplace is one in which people feel safe enough to experiment, to make mistakes, to challenge, to share information, and to support each other. It's a place where employees are prepared to give the manager and the company the "benefit of the doubt." None of this can happen if the individual does not feel cared about. Relationships are the glue that holds all great workplaces together. The manager just sets the tone.

Do great managers find it strange to care about people they might have to fire one day? Definitely not. The best managers define "caring" as "setting each person up for success." They know there will be times when it also means letting someone go, because they know that if the organization cannot provide employees with a role in which they will succeed, firing them is actually a caring thing to do. It may not seem like it at the time, but they feel encouraged by the fact that employees will be free to find other roles that are a better fit for them in the long run.

Great managers and supervisors genuinely care about the people they work with and treat them as the individuals that they are. This includes getting a true sense of satisfaction out of seeing employees grow and succeed—even if an employee's accomplishments surpass those of the manager.

Additionally, the way that employees perceive the organization they work in is filtered through their experiences with their direct managers.

At the same time, great managers know that caring about employees does not necessarily mean going out to dinner with them, inviting them over to their house, or letting them in on all the details of their personal lives. That style works well for some managers but not for others. What works for *all great managers* is finding a way to let each employee know that they genuinely care about her success. For these great managers, caring is about *investment,* not familiarity. Paying attention is what this is all about.

Great managers do not use "steps" to build relationships. They understand that relationships cannot be forced. There are, however, some things they do to form the right climate for trusting relationships. Here is their advice:

• **Do not fake it.** If as a manager you don't care about your people, you shouldn't try to persuade them that you do. Either get a partner who does care about the person or get out of management.

• **Tell them.** You will have to pick your moments and use the style that fits you, but it can be very powerful to say out loud to each of your direct reports, one by one, "I care about your success." Do not assume that they know.

• **Individualize.** Feeling understood is a very powerful emotion. Ask your people some basic questions about their strengths, their expectations, what kind of recognition they like, and how often they like to get together to discuss progress. Get to know your people.

• **Be consistent.** You do not have to treat everyone the same way—each person has a different style with a wide range of needs—but you do have to be consistent in the following. Evaluate each person on performance; try to set each person up for success. Follow through on your commitments because consistency leads to trust, and trust is the foundation of caring.

> I have a friend who, like me, manages about a dozen people at a factory. His place manufactures refrigerator parts; mine builds microchips. When we compare "styles," we differ completely—but both our work groups are people with terrific performers. My friend throws a big picnic in June and an even bigger Christmas party in December to which everyone in his group is invited. They all attend because it's like going home. He tells them to bring their kids and cameras; he gives out inexpensive fun gifts to everyone, and because he is also so accessible all his people feel valued and cared for.
>
> But I'm different. I could no more take one employee out to dinner offsite than I could sprout wings and fly. To me, work relationships belong at work. But that doesn't mean that I ignore my people. I could never do that. What I do is get to know them by their personalities. Some like a literal pat on the back. Some respond to a smile and a thumbs-up. Others like to be spoken to privately, while their colleagues enjoy praise in front of an audience. However I tell them I care—and I do—they know that I mean it. We're as connected as my friend is with his people.

6. Find the right fit.
Here's what the best managers do to invest in the development of the members in their team:

- They help employees differentiate between talent, which occurs naturally and cannot be created, and both skills (the "how-to" of a job) and knowledge (factual or experiential)—each of which can be learned.

- They are innovative in terms of titles and money, and they help people grow within their field of strengths, even if that means bucking the corporate policy on titles and compensation.
- They use trial periods. In most organizations it is hard to let people take control of their careers. If they experiment by taking on new roles that do not work out, they are not admired for trying to learn more about their strengths and weaknesses. Instead they are labeled as "failures." The best managers avoid this problem by letting people try out new roles, having first agreed that they will sit down to review how things are going in a certain period of time. If everything is going great, the employee stays put. But if either the employee or the manager feels the new role is not a good fit, the employee can go back to the previous role without any shame. And though it can be difficult to coordinate these trial periods (the questions of who is going to stand in for the employee during the trial and what happens to this person if the employee comes back are usually raised), the best managers find a way to do it.

Said the manager of a data collection and processing organization:

> One of the women who does data entries in my section raised her own bar. She said she wanted to try for half a million entries a month. She made it. Then she aimed for one million a month, and accomplished that, too. Eventually she was doing 3.4 million entries a month— and the percentage of errors kept decreasing. You know what she said to me? "Every time I raise the bar I get a better definition of who I am."

"Lifetime employability" is the term *du jour* in lieu of the concept of "lifetime employment." Where great managers are concerned, that takes on a new definition. Employing people for life is the goal—because they will keep developing in their jobs. That's what growth is really all about—seeing employees' value grow with their progress.

7. Let people be heard.
Nothing is more demoralizing to employees than being excluded from being able to express opinions about major decisions that directly affect their work. Managers know that the quickest way to spur feelings of irrelevance and insignificance is to hand down decisions that affect employees without getting their input first.

Why do employees say that their opinions do not count? There are two reasons:

1. Opinions aren't being recognized by the right person. A manager is not always the best audience. Sometimes employees want their voices to be heard by the manager's own boss, or by employees in another department. Maybe they prefer their peers. Finding the right audience for them is vital. Good managers always ask their employees who the best person is.
2. The manager doesn't always have to agree with what employees say, or follow their suggestions, but a good manager always asks their opinions. Also, managers are honest. If a decision has already been made, they explain why. Straightforward explanations don't function solely as a communication builder; they are also respect boosters. That's another reason why great managers never dismiss an opinion: It's the quickest way to achieve less-than-committed work, anger, and distrust.

The manager of a hospital laboratory recalled:

I had quite a highly charged emotional situation on my hands. Ten people are in my group, and they were divided about how to determine seniority. Some felt only the time spent at our place should count; others believed that total past experience should be factored in. However, they felt that the decision should not be mine alone. They wanted the head of the company to make the decision. I realized it was the right thing to do and told them so. I gave them my point of view—that all past experience should count—but I also understood the concerns of people who worked at our place for a long time who were worried about others coming in and getting bigger salaries and better benefits. In the end the decision was addressed directly to all the employees and explained. Some grumbled but they accepted the decision because their feelings were respected.

8. Help each person find meaning.

Good managers believe that a part of their jobs is bringing the company's purpose or mission down to size. They do this by explaining it to each person in a form that each individual can relate to. That way all employees can find some connection between the organization's values and their own. Here's how managers do it:

- Clarify the organization's purpose. Different companies use various words for "purpose," such as "mission," "vision," and "core values." Whatever the word, the key question is, "What does this company hold up to be important?" A company may value profit, customer service, creativity, or all three. Whatever its priorities, it is a requirement for the manager to have a clear sense of how this overall idea may be expressed in the language of every team member.
- Help employees find the link between their own values and those of the company. Values vary among employees. Some get excited by competition, others attach importance to service, while others highly regard technical compe-

tence. Whatever their value system, it is the manager's job to try to link the company's purpose to an employee's role. Obviously, a manager cannot do this unless he knows what each team member values. Great managers learn this by asking and observing. At the same time they make sure that "strategy" is never confused with "purpose." The latter is the constant heartbeat of a company, the power that defines what the company is and the impact it intends to have. Strategy provides the changing answers to the question, "How will we get to where we want to go?" Managers emphasize how new strategies support the broader purpose. Managers help individuals link their roles and values to the overall purpose of the organization.

Said the manager in the public relations division of a pharmaceutical company:

One of the people in my sector, a young man who had started working there about six months before, walked up to me one day and said, "I wish I knew what I was doing here." This really startled me, because he performed his job—doing daily recaps of progress on new drugs via e-mail to our employees—very well. When I asked him what he meant, he said, "I don't see how what I do contributes; I understand how all the researchers can make an impact, and I know that the company values life. But where do I fit in?"

I told him that his creative contribution—he could take scientific information and make it accessible to everyone, which was appreciated by a lot of people who didn't sit behind microscopes all day—did make a difference. He transformed heavy-duty technical information into interesting bits of easily digested information. In that way he made the research accessible, which meant that a lot of people without advanced medical degrees—like me—could understand it. When I told

him that the scientists couldn't do what he did, that
their creativity didn't include what he did, his perspective changed. Sometimes, what is so clear to you isn't
clear to an employee. Do both of yourselves a favor: Tell
them how their contribution fits into the bigger picture.

9. We're all in this together.
Great managers clarify the definition of "quality" and make
sure that employees and customers share the same vision of
what that means. Therefore, everyone in a work group must
understand how the customer defines "quality" and agree
with it. Another factor considered is how the company
chooses to measure quality. Does everyone in the work
group understand and agree with the company's definition of
"quality performance"? If everyone doesn't agree, they find
out why.

Great managers identify the affiliation of their team members to quality, regardless of the operational definition. One
problem that affects this commitment is the question of
whether or not every individual plays the right roles within
the team.

The best teams are characterized by a common understanding of the value of each team role, where each individual is positioned to play the part that fits best. Individuals
who don't feel committed to quality work may be wedged
between strengths and job expectation. It is the manager's responsibility to get them unstuck.

That's why many organizations fumble in their attempt to
convey their commitment to quality. By defining "quality" as
"the absence of defects or mistakes," management forces
employees to cover up mistakes or problems as fast as they
can, with as little exposure as possible. In the best workplaces, however, managers realize that human beings make
mistakes, and learn by correcting—not hiding—them. In
these open companies "quality" is defined as "the process
employees use to recognize a problem and figure out its so-

lution." In these cases employees also learn a critical lesson: Customer engagement can increase if responsibility for a problem is taken and a positive approach to solving it is offered. Within the work group quality problems are viewed as challenges to improve a product or service, which will build customer engagement.

Another problem related to commitment to quality is cooperation, where all departments support one another. Often employees say that their co-workers are not committed to turning out quality work, and that other departments may not be giving them the support they need. Outstanding managers try to identify the problems and raise them for discussion. They often lead the charge to pull the two departments together so that the problems can be resolved. This is never easy, but employees always expect the manager to tackle this problem.

The supervisor of a hospital lab said,

Conflict between departments was running high here. My people felt that one of the other departments wasn't as efficient as it could be. The opposing personnel heard about it, and a major confrontation took place. When I asked my employees individually what the problems were, each answered slightly differently. One said that delays were a problem; another said it was accuracy. A third said it was sharing information. Each of these led to the same place: lesser patient care. I spoke to the manager of the other department, and he said he was getting the same complaints about my department from his people. The solution was to sit everyone down and clear the air. It turned out that the departments were trying to compete with one another instead of support each other. They had lost sight of the big picture: Illness and injury were what they were competing against, not each other. Shifting the focus back to where it belonged helped a lot.

10. You'll be there when I need you.

In the perspective of great managers, human beings are most productive when employees cooperate with one another, when they combine efforts, and when they do not have to waste time watching their backs. Great managers understand their team members' need to feel that they can trust the people around them.

Friendship is the gateway to trust, and best-friendship is the proof of that reliance. Therefore, top managers encourage employees to form and sustain genuine workplace friendships, because these relationships increase the amount of shared trust among team members—and this, in turn, increases the productivity of the workplace.

Great managers who observe the benefits of best-friendships know that they're the glue holding members of a work group together. This is so decisive a component that it can determine whether an employee will leave an organization or stay with it.

What can managers do to nurture friendship at work? While they cannot force it, managers can foster an environment where friendships are encouraged. Some ideas include social events "beyond the building," including carpooling or ride sharing, book clubs, fishing trips, bowling leagues, study groups—whatever interests they share. Great managers regularly allocate time to provide an opportunity for team members to get to know one another. One example of this is a "focus on you" session, where each team member gets the chance to share with fellow members their interests, hobbies, plans, and goals outside the organization.

The manager of a furniture store's living room department told us:

> When Jeff started working [here] he was kind of a loner. It was tough for him, because the rest of us had been here for a while and knew each other pretty well. So we all went out to dinner together a couple of times, and

someone mentioned that he liked soccer. Jeff said that he enjoyed it, too, and had played on the varsity team in college. Soon after they went to a game together, and after that they always compared teams and scores at work. They had a language all their own, about international players and teams and all kinds of information that they found fascinating. What I found fascinating was Jeff's demeanor. He had more of a spark and extra enthusiasm. At the end of the day he and his friend would compare sales and customers. Both of them improved their numbers, too. Interesting, isn't it?

Building a strong workplace where the employees' strengths are nurtured and utilized to drive great outcomes is done one work group at a time. The larger the number of truly great managers you have, the stronger your organization, the more you will grow and succeed. But who determines the conditions for great managers? Who defines the playing field in which great managers are being attracted, focused, and developed? The starting point there is the organization's leadership. They define the rules of the game, the focus points of the organization, and the broad conditions under which each team operates. So how can leaders begin to incorporate these critical human capital issues into their lives on a daily basis? This requires a separate discussion, and a separate book, perhaps. To kick off this discussion, however, Gallup has developed a list* of probing questions that will enable discussion around the many facets of leadership.

These items are intended to draw attention to the human potential issues that directly effect the outcomes of any successful organization. In reviewing these items, you will clearly see that they delve into areas that demand clarity and intentional focus. These queries should be addressed within leadership retreats, meetings, and planning sessions.

*Copyright © 2002 The Gallup Organization.

These items address four broad areas of Gallup Path Management: Leadership, Finance, Strategy, and Workplace. Some of the items are listed as "Roundtable," which indicates the need for all participants to respond. Otherwise individual questions should be drawn and answered by individuals.

Below is a sampling of the hundred-plus questions by category. For a full list go to the *Gallup Management Journal* Web site (http://www.gallupjournal.com) and visit the "Follow this Path" site.

Leadership
- When selecting someone to join your team, which talents or qualities will you not live without?
- When hiring, what are some absolutes in your decision?
- How do you align individuals' expectations with your organizational/ team strategy?

Finance
- Ask each person in the room to write down what their definition of "wealthy" is.
- Ask each person to reveal their feelings about stock options, and whether they understand these options.

Strategy
- I can't imagine a world without _____.
- Please name three associates (not at the table) whom we all need to assure have emotional insurance policies. (Roundtable)
- How much face time have you had with clients in the last year?
- Do you want more, or less?
- In what capacity?
- As exec committee members, how much time should we spend with clients?
- How much should we involve our clients in new product development—more or less than we currently do?

Workplace

Expectations
- How do you drive others' performance through expectations?
- How tightly do you hold to expectations?
- When do you raise the high bar?

Opportunity
- Pick three people and tell them what they do best.

11. Look at how far you have come.

All employees need feedback to know how much they have grown. Wanting to know that they contributed to their team, they yearn for signs to track their progress. Great managers, inspired feedback givers, appreciate that an important part of their job is to help employees see the signs of their own progress. Instead of relying on once-a-year performance appraisals, they are constantly on the lookout for chances to point out even the smallest growth increments in each person. For the best managers, this is business as usual.

Our study reveals that there are as many styles of giving feedback as there are managers. Each one finds the style that fits best. Here are a few simple methods shared by the world's outstanding managers:

• **Holding regular one-on-one meetings.** Impromptu feedback can certainly happen—in the hall, in the car on the way back from a meeting—but structured feedback is more potent. Managers fashion a review that serves as a template for all members and meet with each person, depending on the specific work circumstances. Feedback is predominantly focused on individual progress and a review of personal strengths.

• **Recording each person's successes.** Great managers notice and share these among the team members as a combination of feedback and recognition. This happens in real time—that is, right after the action or event takes place. It's like an instant "picture" that describes what the person did.

• **Asking employees to track their own learning.** One of the most powerful initiatives of outstanding managers is to urge all team members to record their learning experiences and accomplishments. This can be as simple as a blank sheet of paper or as formal as a printed "Journal of Performance"—whichever best fits an organizational or managerial style. The point is to encourage all employees to identify and then record their own progress, thus making it theirs alone.

• **Starting the year with a "discovery" review,** in which all employees are queried about their individual objectives and how to assess them, and their individual strengths and how they will use them. Then short, future-focused development meetings each quarter are set up. At these times managers ask about employees' main focus for the following quarter and the strategies each person plans to employ to get there. They always ask what help employees need to realize their objectives. Every performance review, therefore, starts by defining outcomes.

After evaluations take place, great managers are able to answer the following questions about every one of their employees:

- What do they enjoy the most about their current work experience?
- What did they enjoy most about their previous work experience?
- What attracted them to the organization? What keeps them there?
- What are their talents, skills, and knowledge?
- What are their goals for their current roles?
- How often do they like to discuss their progress?
- Are they people who tell how they feel or must they be asked?
- What are their personal goals or commitments?
- What was the best praise or recognition they ever received?
- What were the most productive relationships they have enjoyed with a manager? What made them so special?

The manager of a car dealership explained:

Some in my group began developing their own "report" cards. They keep monthly accounts of how many people come in, how many cars they sold, and so on. Then they review the past six months, and they can see how they are doing. They tell me they learn a lot by doing this: what they are capable of, what they need to work on, and what they want to learn. Also, it's affirming to see how much they've accomplished in a short period of time.

12. Organizations learn through their people.
The chance to learn more means different things to different people. Some employees see it as training classes and seminars. Others think of promotions and increased responsibilities. For some others it might denote special projects or assignments. Before tackling this question, great managers investigate. They learn how each employee defines personal "opportunities."

Great managers know that there is more to learning than skills training in the classroom. For example, employees can learn by spending some time in a debriefing after a project has been completed. A summation of what they remember going well and not so well, it makes for a very valuable exercise. It creates an awareness of emotional states, both of the employee and of the customer.

Similarly, employees can learn fundamentals of a particular activity from other team members. They can also be taught through internal presentations or by spending some time every month with a mentor. Reading a recommended book and writing down a few new ideas works, too.

According to great managers, the responsibility for finding occasions for employees to learn and therefore grow is shared. The finest managers realize that they can never teach anyone anything. All they can do is fashion the kind of envi-

ronment in which employees can learn. Managers view it as
their responsibility to provide a range of learning options
and to lay the ground rules for how and when they can select them. It is *the employees'* responsibility to select from
these options. It is also their responsibility to keep track of
what they have learned.

To help accomplish this sensible objective, great managers
make a real effort to know their people in order to understand individual strengths, talents, and skills. That means listening to what employees say about why they accepted their
roles, what keeps them there, what kind of relationships they
need in order to be most productive, the kind of recognition
they prefer, and where they aim to go in the organization.

Superior managers and employees alike are never completely satisfied with the status quo; they always seek new,
more effective ways to do things.

The marketing manager of a nonprofit organization related:

One of my employees came to me after an especially demanding experience arranging a yearly conference that is
very heavily attended, with an international attendance.
She coordinated reservations, our displays and materials,
and set up several meetings, which was complicated because many of the attendees wanted to sit in on a number
of presentations from other organizations. After it was
over she told me it was an enormous learning experience
for her because of the international factor. "I really had to
listen carefully to what people were saying," she told me,
"and not only because of the different accents. I saw that
cultural differences were present and had to be taken into
account if I wanted to connect with people successfully. At
the end of the day, everything comes down to getting the
particular kind of attention you need."

The Q^{12} Works

Just listen to what the CEO of a large bank had to say about it:

> When we started this process [Q^{12}] we took it as a goal, something like being one of the one hundred best companies to work for. But after seeing the linkages to business results, it has evolved into a business philosophy, so getting an award became secondary. Doing the right thing is our primary objective. And it is the right thing because it makes great financial sense.

And here's what the manager responsible for over a hundred very successful teams made up of more than three thousand employees has to say about it.

Gallup: How do your best managers create and sustain that level of engagement with their employees?

By sincerely listening and caring about what makes each individual "tick" to help push them to new heights of performance, and consequently, retention and engagement. Also . . . by encouraging and creating teams that build off each other and create multiplicity and lifelong friendships, versus a bunch of individual achievers who care only about themselves.

DO WHAT THE GREAT MANAGERS DO

If you want great employees, do what superlative managers do: Engage them. Responding to their emotional needs builds trust and a comfort level. When people feel comfortable, it's logical that they will spend more time focused on work and less on watching their backs. And when you are trusted, your people will want to work harder for you. That's why you should:

- Focus on employees' strengths and manage around their weaknesses.
- Hold people accountable for achieving defined outcomes—using whatever style fits their strengths.
- Acknowledge that the success of the Q^{12} is heavily influenced by the manager.
- Build on strengths and don't stop the process.
- Evaluate the performance, never the person.
- Try to bring out what God left in, instead of trying to put in what God left out.

By realizing what managing to develop and sustain engaged employees means, you have taken the fifth step on The Gallup Path.

CHAPTER 6

Emotional Economics, Part I

"My organization began using emotional economics as a leading indicator of growth and profitability a few years ago," said the CEO of one of the top retailers in the United States. He was one of the many people interviewed for this book.

Gallup: How did you first come into contact with the metrics of employee and customer engagement?

As you can imagine, when I first heard about these, I was very reluctant—you may say skeptical—to the entire idea of "soft numbers," because in my mind all the employee surveys that I had seen hadn't yielded any valuable information that could be applied for decision making. Every time it was like "here's more bad news" without really offering any type of solution on what to do to impact the real problems of our company. A lot of it had to do with not having a yardstick to measure and compare ourselves to other companies and track our progress.

Gallup: Why were you interested in The Gallup Path?

The first thing that crossed my mind was the fact that they had a very robust database, some reliable yardstick against which we could compare ourselves. The second thing that I liked is the perspective of the local culture issue at the level of individual work groups. I felt relieved to find out that the employee issues are not really a monster, but really a work group set of issues that can be effectively managed; it was like a lightbulb went on in my mind when I saw that. At that moment I decided to give it a try.

Gallup: What did you learn from this first experience?

Something that I will never forget: I saw that we were no different from other companies in that inside our organization we had the world's best and the world's worst cultures at the work group level. So I felt that there we had an opportunity. The second thing that impressed me was to find the linkages [from] the good and the bad results to the financial outcomes that drive our business performance. There were unequivocal signs that these results were linked to our margins, our growth, and ultimately the annual performance of our company. From there on, I felt committed to tracking and studying these numbers.

Gallup: How did you apply these metrics?

When I saw that the best-scoring teams were also the most profitable, I said to myself, "Maybe these scores are the right cure for the issues that keep bothering me." So we tried to align the average and the low-performing groups in our company to the conditions that distinguished our best teams. Intuitively, I felt that I had always known these teams had something special going for them, but now I had hard data, and we could then move to set the right expectations of performance.

Gallup: What are these expectations?

First, we hold our managers responsible for upholding and improving their work group scores. Second, we expect every employee—at all levels—to try to make a contribution that affects these numbers. Here, we all do it. All the way from the CEO to the part-time clerk use the same consistent language. And we also expect to be within the top 25 percent of the worldwide database within five years.

Gallup: What are the incentives that make you try that hard?

There is only one incentive that works for me, and that is the financial state of our company. In all honesty, I believe in using these metrics because they helped me save this company $250 million—and add a comparative amount to the top line—in the course of the first year I tried. Ever since it keeps paying off. This is the real motivator for me.

The Proof Is Here

Over and over again, hundreds of independent Gallup studies, representing dozens of companies in dozens of industries, highlight a constant in the fluctuating economics of organizations. There is a direct, causal link between the twelve conditions in the workplace and virtually every important business outcome of an organization. This holds for industries worldwide, no matter what their size or function.

It turns out that those business units that scored high in the Q^{12} consistently performed better than those that scored low did.

Here's why. The twelve conditions have a statistically important impact on the productivity, safety, retention, and profitability of an organization. According to the 2002 Meta-Analysis, the twelve conditions have a statistically important impact on the productivity, safety, retention, and profitability of an organization. Business units in the top half of employee engagement (compared with business units in the bottom half) show on average:

- 86 percent higher success rate on customer metrics.
- 70 percent higher success in lowering turnover.

- 70 percent higher success rate in productivity.
- 44 percent higher success rate in profitability.
- 78 percent higher success rate in safety figures.

The studies reveal something even more dramatic: Their impact is accentuated by the wide variation in the levels of employee *engagement* and *disengagement* coexisting within a single company. This range is caused by the relative presence of engaged, not-engaged, and actively disengaged employees. These groups, taken together, form the "engagement index."

The Engagement Index

When this index was developed in 2000, the idea was to use it to determine just how large a proportion of the employed population were actually uncommitted to their jobs, that is, "emotionally unemployed."

We started thinking that organizations are composed of two competing forces: one that was positive and engaged, and one that was negative and disengaged. It would follow that the conflict between them would foster immense tension in the work environment. But when we further explored the combination of scores in the twelve conditions, three—not two—distinct groups of employees were apparent. Please note that these are neither psychological profiles nor definitions that just make good conceptual sense. Rather, they stem from mutually exclusive combinations of scores in the twelve conditions—and they really make a substantially different impact on the business outcomes of an organization as they utilize the emotional incentives of engagement.

THE ENGAGED

The first group, the engaged, are the employees who pack the biggest punch on all the important business outcomes that were considered, that is, productivity, customer retention, low turnover, safety, profitability, and growth. Gallup studies have confirmed that these employees are involved in generating *all* of an organization's profits and customer engagement. Collectively, these employees represent the positive economic force that fuels an organization's profitable growth.

The engaged employee profile:

- Use their talents every day.
- Consistent levels of high performance.
- Natural innovation and drive for efficiency.
- Intentional building of supportive relationships.
- Clear about the desired outcomes of their role.
- Emotionally committed to what they do.
- Challenge purpose to achieve goals.
- High energy and enthusiasm.
- Never run out of things to do, but create positive things to act on.
- Broaden what they do and build on it.
- Commitment to company, work group, and role.

Potential pothole: Engaged employees can fall into a comfort zone and stop stretching to new performance levels.

That's what happened to Ana, a claims adjuster at a health insurance company. After five years of ever-better performance, she topped out. Her work didn't slide, but it stopped improving. Her supervisor realized something must be holding her back and asked her if anything was wrong. "I guess I feel that this is as good as I can be," Ana told her. "I always thought I'd excel at this job, and I am." But when her supervisor asked her if she found her work as appealing as she usually did, Ana shrugged her shoulders. "Not really; but after five years isn't that to be expected?" Then her supervisor asked her what she would like to accomplish next. Ana thought for a bit and replied, "I would like to learn a more involved computer program. A couple of years ago I didn't think I could handle it, but I feel that I'm ready for it now."

What Ana's supervisor did was help Ana stretch to the next level where she could improve her performance—and she made it happen through an emotional connection.

With engaged employees, the manager's role is to:

- Make them aware of their individual strengths. Do this by providing continuous feedback on how individual strengths are being used.
- "Clear the path" so that a person can do what she does best without unnecessary distractions.
- Form a relationship that an employee wants to stretch for. Build trust by showing your commitment to his success.
- Challenge each person within areas of her distinctive strengths.
- Focus upon particular skills and knowledge in order to build talent into strength.
- Give each employee ownership and creation of his outcomes. Suggest strategies to get to those results and point out progress along the way.

THE NOT-ENGAGED

The difference between this group and the engaged is twofold. First, their impact on business outcomes is not as significant. Second, they exhibit gaps in levels of engagement, which makes them less predictable as a group. Some employees may share the values and the mission of their team and organization but lack precision in terms of the expectations of their role. Others may experience the need to employ their talent more directly, while for still others the gap may refer only to the absence of a meaningful relationship with their manager.

The profile of the not-engaged is highly individual and does not reflect that of either a collective group or a company profile. The continued tracking of engagement by Gallup is very encouraging. It shows that many not-engaged employees can be considered "in transit." They are waiting for an opportunity to become fully engaged.

The not-engaged employee profile:

- Meets the basics.
- Confusion, or inability to act with confidence.
- Low-risk responses and commitment.
- No real sense of achievement.
- Possible commitment to organization, but not always to role or work group.
- Will speak frankly about negative views.

Potential pothole: Not-engaged employees can lower the bar so that average is acceptable.

Cliff, whose work as a bank teller was okay—no major mistakes, no customer complaints, no slacking off—didn't push himself to do any more than was necessary. His fellow tellers regarded him as a pretty good colleague: He did his job well and fit in. But whenever there was something extra to do, he wouldn't volunteer for it. Nor would he offer suggestions, as other tellers did, about moving lines faster or implementing new customer incentives.

Then the bank manager sat down with Cliff to get his take on how things were going. "Why? Is there a problem?" Cliff wanted to know. When he was reassured that his work was going well, Cliff relaxed a bit. When the manager asked him how he saw himself in his role, Cliff was taken aback. "I'm a bank teller," he replied. "What else am I supposed to be?" The manager pointed out that each teller was a representative of the bank, and that making customers feel that they, and their money, were being looked after carefully was crucial. There were a lot of other banks in the area, and competition was stiff. "I know that," Cliff answered. "But what can I do? I don't feel comfortable chatting customers up when I'm depositing and cashing checks. I never did." When asked what he really felt comfortable doing, Cliff said, "I check mortgage rates every day, not only ours but competing ones. That kind of information fascinates me. I can see how it can affect a family. It makes a difference, you know?"

The manager picked up on this and suggested that Cliff try the mortgage desk for a couple of months to see how it worked out. That's what Cliff did—and two years later he is the most effective mortgage lender the bank has.

By seeking and recognizing the emotional connection that Cliff needed to excel, the manager found a way to engage him in his work.

With the not-engaged, the manager's role is to:

- Review the demands of each role.
- Clarify the desired outcomes of these roles.
- Tweak the fit to the role if necessary. If you have to, move people into new roles that better fit their talent combination.
- Use a direct dialogue so that you can get the feedback you need to address the problem.
- Measure progress toward outcomes by rating the performance—never the person.

THE ACTIVELY DISENGAGED

The third group represents real trouble. The analyses conducted by Gallup show that this group accounts for most of the waste in terms of lost workdays, incredibly high safety costs, higher levels of turnover, low productivity, and customer defection. Collectively, these employees represent a negative economic force actively at work within organizations. They exist at all levels, in all functions and teams. To a large extent actively disengaged employees undo the great work of the engaged employees, effectively canceling it out. Collectively, this group stagnates the growth of a company and represents the most significant challenge to its profitability. They are living and breathing obstacles to meeting customer requirements.

Interestingly, the level of disengagement may not be due to individuals' choice but rather to serious gaps in the fulfillment of their emotional needs. But for some, the problem may be as simple as being too talented to work with an unfit manager. The problem for most organizations is that, on average, a full 30 percent of the actively disengaged workers still plan to be with the company a year hence.

The actively disengaged employee profile:

- Normal reaction starts with resistance.
- Low trust.
- "I'm okay, everyone else is not."
- Inability to move from the problem to the solution.
- Low commitment to company, work group, and role.
- Isolation.
- Won't speak frankly about negative views but will act out frustration, either overtly or covertly.

Potential pothole: Actively disengaged employees will want to be told what to do, with no recognition of the desired outcome.

"Tell me what you want and I'll do it." That was the statement that Tad made to his supervisor at the computer supply store every day. So every day the supervisor had to tell him to move certain merchandise to be more visible, approach customers in a particular way, and provide the information they needed.

The fact that sales were important was not beyond Tad; he understood the cause and effect of selling. But why he had to deal with customers in that particular way eluded him. "They come in because they need stuff; they come because we have what they want. Just how far do I have to go with them?" he'd ask.

After three months of dealing with Tad's attitude, the supervisor knew that Tad wasn't helping the store; he was hurting it. He asked Tad to come in early so that they could figure out what to do. "Do you feel that your job is right for you?" the supervisor asked him. "Because if it's not we should think about other jobs that would be a better fit. You know a lot about computers but you give the impression that every person walking in here should know as much as you do."

"I guess that is how I feel. I don't mean to make people uncomfortable. It's just that I'm more comfortable with the computers than I am with people." With that, the supervisor asked him, "Would you prefer to work on the computers, installing extra software and fixing them?"

"Absolutely. It would be a relief. Then I could see what I was doing, really see the effect."

By realizing that Tad could not establish an emotional connection with customers, his supervisor helped find the right role for him.

With the actively disengaged,
the manager's role is to:

- Address the problem as soon as possible.
- Talk to the person involved, rather than other people, about how to address the problem.
- Use direct, up-front language. Present the real problems to avoid confusion.
- Help the person understand that she has to move out of the problem and into the solution.
- Review the talent fit for the role. Be honest with yourself and the person involved. Act swiftly to find the "right" talent/role fit.
- Create trust by talking more about outcomes than about the steps needed to get there.

The Index Mirror

How employees see themselves in the index also offers insight. The *Gallup Management Journal* reports that engaged employees are fifteen times more likely than actively disengaged workers to recommend their company as a place to work and sixteen times more likely to say that their current role employs their individual strengths. Additionally, they are three times more likely to be satisfied with their current compensation plans and benefits and to spend their entire career at their present company.

The level of engagement also affects the self-assessment of quality of life. Engaged employees are eleven times more likely than their actively disengaged comrades to indicate that they are extremely satisfied with their current company as a place to work. They are four times more likely to evaluate their condition of life as excellent, and twice as likely to say that they are extremely satisfied with their personal lives.

In contrast, actively disengaged employees feel much less

confident. They are nine times more likely than engaged employees to say that they are less secure about their jobs than they were a year before. They are three times more likely to indicate that their stress-related work has caused them to behave poorly with their families, and twice as likely to indicate that they have less time to do the things they want to do.

So any organization that believes that employees leave their personal concerns behind them when they come to work, and park their work concerns at the office door at the end of the day are doing their employees—and themselves—a big disservice.

Engagement tends to vary in terms of length of employment as well. On average, in the first six months of employment, 38 percent of employees are engaged, 50 percent are not-engaged, and only 12 percent are actively disengaged. But from the next six months to three years later, the proportion of engaged employees drops to 27 percent, the not-engaged increase marginally to 55 percent, and the proportion of actively disengaged rises significantly to 18 percent. From three to ten years of employment, the proportions of engagement and disengagement balance in a ratio of 1:1 at 22 percent each; after ten years of employment, the proportion of the engaged drops to 20 percent, while the actively disengaged increases to 23 percent.

And even though the Gallup study shows that the proportions of engaged and disengaged employees do not vary significantly by type of industry, there is one kind of organization that reports a significantly larger proportion of disengaged employees: the government sector. Here, the proportion of disengaged employees increases to 29 percent.

When dollars and cents are tallied, the cost of disengagement is severe. Using very conservative estimates, our study shows that on average, the lost-productivity cost of active disengagement represents a full $3,400 per $10,000 of salary. For an employee who earns an annual salary of $30,000, the cost is $10,200; if the salary is $50,000, the cost is $17,000, and so on, all the way up to the executive committee. At that high salary level, the savings generated just through a zero-disengagment policy would be more substantial than the savings accounted for by all other cost reduction efforts combined.

The multiyear research on employee engagement at Gallup also revealed that on average and across job types, women are more engaged in their work. And while the three levels of engagement are somewhat changeable, moving from not-engaged to engaged is the most consistent pattern from the first year the Q^{12} is introduced.

Employee Engagement: The National Index

In October 2000 Gallup first reported the proportion of the engaged, the not-engaged, and the actively disengaged in the U.S. economy. *The national trend indicates that only about one-third of the workplace in the United States is engaged, while approximately one-fifth is actively disengaged.*

Since then, these estimates have been available quarterly (you can get them in the *Gallup Management Journal* or you can read them on the front page of the *Wall Street Journal*). This is the macro picture affecting the economy and the competitiveness of each country.

To demonstrate how dramatic the engagement index is on the American economy, consider this: The latest figures show that only 30 percent of the U.S. workforce consists of engaged employees. Over half—54 percent—are not-engaged, while 16 percent are actively disengaged. The study of these three groups is important because it represents a continuing benchmark against which individual companies can compare themselves. It also reveals the competitive position of one national economy against others, particularly its most important trade partners and competitors. And it can be used to measure the impact of important events on the productivity and health of the workplace.

The side-by-side existence of engagement and disengagement within the same organization is a global problem. In 2001 Gallup conducted a national benchmark of the engagement index in a host of countries. The numbers are sobering:

- In Canada, 24 percent are engaged, 60 percent are not-engaged, and 16 percent are actively disengaged.
- In Chile, 25 percent are engaged, 62 percent are not-engaged, and 13 percent are actively disengaged.
- In Germany, 16 percent are engaged, 69 percent are not-engaged, and 15 percent are actively disengaged.
- In Great Britain, 17 percent are engaged, 63 percent are not-engaged, and 20 percent are actively disengaged.
- In Singapore, 6 percent are engaged, 76 percent are not-engaged, and 17 percent are actively disengaged.
- In Japan, 9 percent are engaged, 72 percent are not-engaged, and 19 percent are actively disengaged.
- In France, 9 percent are engaged, 63 percent are not-engaged, and 28 percent are actively disengaged.

Interestingly, the most important differences among countries don't reside in their relative numbers of engaged employees, but in how many of their workers are actively disengaged.

Employee disengagement costs money. Using the most conservative scenarios, Gallup has calculated that the cost to the U.S. economy of actively disengaged employees is in the range of $254 to $363 billion annually. This amount is larger than the U.S. budget for either education or national defense.

Still, with a mere fraction of engaged employees the U.S. economy manages to thrive. Imagine how much it could grow and accomplish by doubling the number of these pivotal workers. Great organizations can boast that close to 50 percent of their employees are actively engaged.

The Engagement Ratios

If employee engagement and disengagement represent opposite active forces in the workplace, with one of these commanding the financial outcomes of the organization, the compelling question is which one of these ends up winning. This issue sparked our initial interest in the study of engagement ratios, which measured the proportion of engaged employees against those of disengaged workers. Fortunately, the research on employee engagement has ballooned over the past few years, and the data are comprehensive enough for us to draw some interesting conclusions.

Studying the trends of employee engagement over the course of several years bolstered our views. This allowed us to draw reliable observations in terms of what happens when organizations institute specific acts of intervention, most notably aligning individual strengths and roles with a great manager. Here are some trends we have observed in our database.

Once the Q^{12} is used, the increase in the number of engaged employees starts to develop in the very short term. Some start at a low of 11 percent of engaged employees, while others may start with a much higher 35 percent, but both can achieve single-digit increases within a single year. Simultaneously, the proportion of disengaged employees decreases—but this component usually takes longer to unfold. There are cases in which organizations start with a proportion of 20 percent or higher of disengaged employees, and this number—gradually but appreciably—comes down to single digits over the course of a five-year period. In Gallup's database the range in the engaged-to-disengaged ratios observed goes from 1:1 to 11:1 when the Q^{12} is implemented.

The numbers tend to vary only in terms of the size of organizations. Engagement is highest (33 percent of employees) at companies with fewer than fifty workers and lowest (22 percent) at companies with more than one thousand employees. Something similar occurs with disengagement: It is lower at companies with fewer than fifty employees (12 percent) and highest at companies with more than one thousand (19 percent).

Here is a sample of amazing success stories:

- A major U.S. retailer saw the proportion of its engaged employees triple in the course of five years.
- A manufacturing firm noticed its proportion of engaged employees rise almost twofold in one year.
- A computer solutions organization became aware of a major increase in its number of engaged employees in a single year (from 24 to 36 percent), while at the same time the proportion of its disengaged workers declined a full 7 percentage points (from 16 to 9 percent).
- A major financial organization observed the proportion of engaged employees increase by a third and its disengaged employees decline by a third in the course of the same two-year period.
- A transportation organization watched its proportion of engaged employees grow an incredible 11 percentage points (from 19 to 30 percent) in only twelve months.

Ultimately, it is the ratio of engaged workers to disengaged that drives the financial outcome of the organization, particularly where active disengagement is concerned. Here's one example involving a network of hospitals. Its figures estimated that in terms of lost workdays, not-engaged employees reported missing 1.9 more days per year than engaged employees did. Disengaged employees missed 4.8 more days than the engaged. This amounted to an excess of 6,026 more days lost due to lack of engagement. At an average cost of

$154 per day each, the network's annualized cost relative just to lost-work days amounted to $928,004. And this is just the tip of the disengagement iceberg. Extra costs due to lower productivity and waste in turnover, shrinkage, and safety were substantial. Add the more hidden but equally real costs of remedial, ineffective, and indiscriminate training and compensation and you can see that the costs of employee disengagement are nothing short of astronomical.

Here's another case from the health care industry. A major chain of hospitals found that, over a two-year period, an increase of 0.2 in its Q^{12} engagement score resulted in a financial improvement per admission of $245.72 in EBIDTA (earnings before interest, depreciation, and taxes). By contrast, if its engagement score declined from year one to year two, its EBIDTA per admission went down an average of $192.98. And this chain also found that its engagement scores predicted higher inpatient ratings of hospital processes in twelve to eighteen months.

Or consider what a $6 billion software organization achieved in just one year. Before implementing the Q^{12}, the proportion of engaged employees was 24 percent; not-engaged employees accounted for 60 percent of the workforce, and actively disengaged employees represented 16 percent. Turnover figures were 7 percent for engaged employees, 13 percent for the not-engaged, and 28 percent for the actively disengaged group. In the course of one year the proportion of engaged employees increased to 36 percent, while the number of actively disengaged employees dropped to 9 percent. By achieving a 4:1 ratio, the company was able to cut turnover in half and, according to its own estimates, save $250 million on the bottom line.

Turn Over a New Policy

Organizations know that turnover is costly. The stats published by The Corporate Leadership Council of the Corporate Executive Board show that the cost of turnover for front-line employees is equal to 0.41 times salary; that of professional associates is equal to 1.77 times salary, and that for managers is 2.44 times salary. So for an organization of ten thousand employees, a 5 percent decrease in employee turnover saves $4 million for front-line employees earning $20,000 a year, $35 million for professional associates earning $40,000 a year, and $97 million for managers earning $80,000 a year.

No wonder that the impact of employee engagement on retention is one of the most widely studied effects.

Take the example of a large retailer with more than 360 stores. The annualized turnover rate of the 10 percent of stores with the highest Q^{12} scores was 49 percent. Collectively, these turnovers cost the retailer $22.3 million per year. But the 10 percent of stores with the lowest Q^{12} scores had a turnover rate of 148 percent—and they cost the company $67.3 million annually.

Naturally, these data caught the executive council's attention. If engagement was independent of geographic location, store size, length of operation, and all other variables, then the question was: "Why not have all stores comply with the requirements of engagement that already exist in our best stores?"

For this retailer, the multimillion-dollar difference was not considered an inevitable cost of doing business. On the contrary, the retailer embarked on a continuing effort to eradicate disengaged stores by using the Q^{12} conditions—and the effort paid off.

Another retailer had much the same experience: The 10 percent of its stores with top Q^{12} scores experienced a turnover problem of 52 percent, representing $17.2 million annually. The 10 percent of stores with bottom Q^{12} scores revealed a turnover problem of 150 percent, at a cost of $53 million annually. At this company something else was going on in terms of compensation claims. The 10 percent of stores with the best Q^{12} scores had compensation claims equal to $85.37 per work group per year, while the 10 percent of stores with the worst Q^{12} scores had compensation claims equal to $42,781.

Even more fascinating numbers emerged. From year one to year two, the 25 percent of stores with the best Q^{12} scores enjoyed an increase in sales over their quotas of 4.56 percent, whereas the 25 percent of stores with the lowest Q^{12} scores presented sales budgets 0.84 percent lower than their established quotas. The difference added up to $120 million.

This company has been able to reduce its internal variation among stores—it now has a lot more "best" and a lot fewer "bad" stores. At the same time it has improved its overall Q^{12} score. In its first year, its overall score fell right in the middle among all the scores in Gallup's database. But by year three the companywide score had jumped twenty places—to level sixty of one hundred. By the fourth year the overall score was at point seventy, which meant that its business units, combined, were among the 30 percent best workplaces in a database of more than 300,000 business units worldwide.

Now take a look at a large organization of more than fifty-five thousand employees that was interested in finding out how to improve its safety record among its more than four hundred business units. From year one to year two it saw some intriguing engagement patterns emerge. In the 25 percent of its business units that had the highest Q^{12} scores, the incidence of accidents dropped 42 percent, the number of lost workdays due to accidents also fell 52 percent, and the insurance costs at these stores dipped 42 percent. Something very different happened at the 25 percent of stores with the bottom Q^{12} scores. The incidence of accidents dropped only

4 percent, the number of days lost due to accidents fell only 2 percent, and the insurance costs actually increased a full 2 percent. The difference accounted for by employee engagement added up to hundreds of millions of dollars.

The New Road

The reporting of the economic impact of engagement on profits and growth has only begun. This study is ongoing at Gallup, and there are numerous areas of hidden impact that remain to be revealed and estimated. But right now the undisputed fact is that employee engagement significantly impacts the ability of an organization to achieve profitable growth.

Since nothing in an organization occurs inside a human vacuum, however, every single event handled by human beings bears the handprint of their engagement.

The challenge is in catching up with the organizations that have already reduced the variation of engagement/disengagement within.

What can companies do to improve their ratio of engagement? First, "think big and act small," because the only way to find the real solutions to problems in the workplace is at the workplace level. The solution already lies inside your own organization, at superior individual workplaces where the outstanding stories of engagement can be identified and applied to the entire organization.

Second, it's time to realize that all problems relating to engagement are directly associated with talent that is either underutilized or ignored. No matter how many percentages are tallied or numbers are crunched, without important relationships among workers and between managers and work groups, engagement cannot happen. This is the first fundamental lesson of emotional economics.

THE DISENGAGEMENT WARNINGS
YOU MUST HEED

The numbers don't lie. You must identify your engaged, not-engaged, and actively disengaged employees, because they make huge impacts on your business every day. And unless your employees become engaged to their work and work group—and stay that way—they won't be able to work to their maximum ability.

If you want to win in an increasingly competitive business world, you must look at your employees as your first line of defense. They can make you—or break you. If you are managing within a typical business environment, the reality is that the majority of the people working with you aren't doing a great job. Many of them are doing such a poor job that they are hurting your business. You probably realize who the less-than-productive people are; now it's time to understand the harm they cause and turn them around. Remember:

• **The majority of employees are not engaged at work.** More than forty-two independent Gallup studies indicate that approximately 75 percent of employees in most companies are not engaged at work.

• **Disengaged employees cost companies hundreds of million of dollars annually.** Employees who are disengaged from their current roles cost companies fortunes in lost revenue, higher turnover, lost workdays, and lower productivity.

• **Remedial training doesn't cure disengagement.** Training is remedial, because the outcome is always average or below-average performance.

• **Companies create waste.** Waste and lost opportunities represented by disengaged employees are pulling your organization down.

- **The longer employees stay with their company, the less engaged they become.** These studies also show that on average, the first year that employees work at an organization is their best. Their level of engagement gradually decreases with tenure. Most of the tenured employees are merely "there" or have turned into ROAD (retired on active duty) kill.

By understanding the economic implications of engaged, not-engaged, and actively disengaged employees, you have taken the sixth step on The Gallup Path.

CHAPTER 7

The Open Highway

The Green Light and the Stop Sign

Whenever Katie needs to replenish her makeup supply, she heads for a particular line of cosmetics at a popular upscale department store:

> It's not that what I use is exclusive to one store; I can buy this particular line of products, which I've been using for years, in several places. The store I go to is a little out of my way, but I don't mind heading there. The reason I go is that I finally found a salesperson—they're called "consultants"—who is fabulous. When I first met her, I was bowled over by her personality. She shook my hand, introduced herself, and did it in the context of a conversation that she was just finishing with another customer.
>
> What I found so pleasant was that this woman—Terry—spoke about herself for a bit. She bemoaned the fact that she was old enough to have a twenty-five-year-old daughter. She griped a bit about her weight. When I told her what I needed, she got it, quickly asked if I wanted anything else—and she didn't try to sell me anything else, which was a relief. She said she

had been representing this product line for eighteen years, and wouldn't think of selling anything else; for her, it would be dishonest. Before I left she reminded me not to forget my gloves. There's no chance I'll forget her, either.

Katie, a customer, experienced an emotional connection with an employee because she received a unique, personalized experience. Because she has established a strong, positive emotional association with the salesperson, the store, and the line of cosmetics, she has become an engaged customer. Her rational reactions may have helped her initially try the products, but it is her emotional response to Terry that will make her buy them again.

Now Katie has a positive emotional memory of her experience.

Tim, who likes to order a very well-known soft drink whenever he goes to a restaurant, has a different story:

I think it's the bubbles that I really get a kick out of; and since champagne on a daily basis is not a possibility, I choose this particular soda. It tastes good. It's everywhere. Or at least almost everywhere. Recently, I went to lunch with a couple of friends, and the restaurant didn't carry this brand. So I ordered its main competitor. You know what? It went down pretty easy. I guess I'm not as good a consumer as I thought. Out of sight, out of mind.

Said his friend Tony:

Something similar happened to me, but with hotels. When we arrive on a business trip, sometimes I find myself saying, "Who cares which one we go to?" After all, it's just a place to stay.

If either Tim or Tony had a really strong positive emotional bond with his preferred brand of soft drink or hotel, he probably wouldn't have settled for a competitor's brand. No emotional connection was made. Thus, these potentially "engaged" customers were lost.

Neither Tim nor Tony has a positive relationship with these brands that resonates in the emotional memory of his experiences.

Our Emotional Memory Is What Counts

For more than a century, conventional wisdom held that all of our learning was driven by one system: our rational memory dictated by our conscious awareness. So when it came to analyzing how our memory works, the assumption was that we retrieve information stored by our rational mind. Today we know that's dead wrong. In the past twenty years, neuroscience has shown us that there are multiple learning and memory systems in our brain, and that our emotional mind works independently from our rational mind. In his acclaimed book *The Emotional Brain,* leading neuroscientist Joseph LeDoux notes the difference by stating that conscious recolleciton is the kind of memory that we have in mind when we use the term "memory" in everyday conversations. Memories of this type can be brought to mind and described verbally.

But there is another type of memory, one that takes place outside of our conscious awareness. This is the memory where we house our emotions, the nonconscious recollection of how we felt at a particular occasion. For example: Think about your last interaction with a customer and ask yourself, of everything that went on in that interaction, what does my customer remember as something worth coming back again for? The product, the service processes, the price paid; but unless I have a precise understanding of how that customer felt, I only have a small fraction of what really counts for the customer to come back again.

In practice the systems that control our emotional memory have been ignored by organizations and, therefore, have not been maximized to engage and retain customers. The implication is that customers know how they are treated, and they are naturally conditioned to use this knowledge in future purchase or usage occasions. But the system that controls their reactions operates outside of their conscious awareness and recollection. So, how organizations reach their emotional memory, impact it, and leave a positive lasting experience is the subject of much deserved attention.

TRY THIS "ROAD" TEST

Read this paragraph and then do it. Close your eyes and think about the last time you visited one of your favorite stores. Review entering the store, looking for merchandise that you liked, reading product information, deciding what to buy, and purchasing the item. If you were returning an item, remember what happened at the customer service counter.

How do you feel about it? Adding all the individual experiences doesn't exactly sum up your overall evaluation of the store. Some things will stand out—some positively, others negatively. Still, your experience is likely to be emotionally colored by your interactions with the people and the store. How you felt about those interactions left a lasting emotional impression.

That's because your emotions are stored separately from your rational ideas or thoughts. While you can think about a store dispassionately, it is impossible to distance yourself from your real emotions about most of the stores you frequent. Every experience is charged with an emotional current. And feelings can change as a result of personal relationships that either build or erode the memory you have of your experiences.

Rational decisions clearly represent only one portion—often a minor one—of choices made. How customers feel about products or services is often determined by their emotional relationship with the people who represent these products or services.

At the Crossroads

While many organizations strive to attract new customers, great organizations operate with a different agenda. They don't stop thinking about their customers after they arrive. They know that customer acquisition is just the initial step, not the ultimate goal. The objective is retaining them—one customer at a time. Great organizations know that, on average, 80 percent of an organization's growth potential lies in existing customers and only 20 percent in new ones. A variety of data dating back to the early 1990s point in this direction. So rather than focusing only on creating new demand or meeting one need, their aim is to attract new customers while keeping and nourishing the customers they already cherish.

Unfortunately, the great organizations stand alone at the fork in this particular road. Very misguided and extremely limited assumptions about what customers value, including their preferences, how they frame alternatives, make purchases, and decide whether to switch or stay have severely affected the growth and profitability of many organizations. And that's not all: Most organizations fail to measure the emotional connection between a company and a customer. This is critically important, because that link establishes an enduring customer relationship.

The combination of these factors created an exclusive focus on attempting to create customer relationships through very traditional methods such as improved products and processes that virtually ignored emotions. These "relationship enhancement" programs did absolutely nothing to shift attention to where it belongs: onto the emotional engagement of customers.

The notion that customers make decisions based only on their conscious awareness and their rational thinking is influenced by a century-old theory of the consumer that reduced mental activity to visible behavior. In the beginning of the twentieth century, economists tried to explain consumers' decisions by "translating" what was subjective (tastes and preferences) into something objective (choices concerning consumption). This brought about a seemingly elegant theory, which continues to influence current assumptions about the customer: the concept of patterns of "revealed preferences."

According to this theory, customer behavior—that is, making purchases and repurchases—is a reflection of the value propositions represented by the different options available in the market. Therefore, each customer simply "makes a choice" by selecting the one option that is judged as being more valuable than the alternatives.

There are two major problems with this convenient theory. First, it fails to explain the mental and emotional processes that take place inside the human mind in the course of making a purchase decision. Discoveries in neuroscience reveal that given the computational limitations of the human mind, it is not the choice itself but the moments of framing the alternatives for choice that really matter. These moments are significantly influenced by feelings and emotions and not just by rational thought.

Customers are emotion-seeking individuals, they make choices to satisfy emotional desires and not merely their rational needs. For example, a couple celebrating an anniversary will limit their options to the restaurants that will deliver the atmosphere they crave. Or a passenger will choose to buy a ticket in person at the train station rather than electronically because he knows that agent at the station personally. He trusts that the agent will answer his questions and ease his worry about getting on the right train at the right time.

The second problem is that the theory assumes humans possess the omniscient power to see and evaluate all possible combinations and select only the one that maximizes a complex "value algorithm." The number and the nature of the difficulties contained in the notion make it almost impossible to understand how customers make choices. Most customers do not aim only for the highest possible rational return. Often they just settle for options that meet their most important emotional expectations.

Additionally, from an operational perspective, organizations have failed because they have been unable to establish a proven link between their customer metrics and the business outcomes that are the company's real goals. Consider the "customer satisfaction" measures that organizations use to try to gauge their customer experiences. Some organizations pledge to "always exceed customer expectations" without being aware that they can exceed expectations only once as the newfound level of service and performance becomes the basic expectation. Most organizations find it hard to improve their level of service even once! Dissatisfied customers, if given a choice, are unlikely to select the same option again. But satisfied customers are also very unreliable. They may declare that they are willing to come back, but often they defect instead.

DO YOU REALLY KNOW YOUR CUSTOMERS?

Until you understand the emotions that drive repurchase behavior—and how to produce them through your employees—your customer research is in need of substantial repair.

Since many organizations assume that customers' decisions are mainly rational, they focus mainly on functional "controllables" (ranging from decreasing the time waiting, to clean uniforms, to the amount of ice in a soft drink) that are easy to manage. However, they have also proven to be relatively unimportant when it comes to engaging and sustaining a customer relationship.

Finally, organizations do themselves and their customers a huge disservice where retention activities are concerned. They tend to rely almost exclusively on solitary actions designed and executed in isolated functional areas within their companies. These are known as "silos" that represent the ways in which a company manages its business, but often misrepresent what is valued by the customer. Silos include marketing, advertising, product development, sales, operations, and customer call centers.

Often customer retention programs become single-touchpoint solutions, like a bank that assumes that friendliness is the direct and sole result of a teller addressing a customer by name.

Or worse, organizations yield to the temptation to script "one-size-fits-all" behaviors in an attempt to standardize a set of behaviors that every employee is supposed to use all the time to address customer issues. "We apologize for the inconvenience but at this time we don't have a way to resolve your problem" is a classic example. These actions are nothing less than an application of techniques that were originally intended to improve the quality of production lines.

But perhaps most troubling of all, most customer retention programs fail to involve the individual front-line employees, who are, for many companies, the pivotal agents of emotional attachment and customer engagement.

Organizations also use interventions that maneuver them in the wrong directions. Among them are:

- Overemphasizing advertising as the most effective method to connect with customers emotionally.
- CRM, or customer relationship management, in which software painstakingly records "intelligence"—personal data—about customers. Technology focused, CRM rarely predicts return behavior. The real problem is that more customer information doesn't mean better information, nor does it assume that an organization is focused on the customer. Also, these databases can easily be copied by competitors.
- Isolated initiatives—that is, complaint bandages wherein a customer is given a perk to cover up a bad experience. Getting an upgrade on a future flight after being bumped from a previous one is a common example.
- Cutting prices, which may attract customers but will in no way assure their return unless competitors fail to match them.
- Various customer satisfaction measurement programs. As all too many organizations have learned, satisfaction is not a bond.

Emphasis in most organizations stays firmly targeted on functional processes (like speeding check-in at a hotel) that require little or no real involvement of front-line employees. It's also important to note that research on the dynamics of customer interactions shows that reducing errors in customer service does not translate into customer engagement. Errors, of course, do inflict damage because they erode confidence, an emotional foundation of a customer relationship.

However, problem handling and resolution very often create engagement because they're often person-to-person processes that reflect established company policies.

Saying It Doesn't Make It So

Only rarely do products and advertising create emotional engagement. Think about the ads you remember; they hinted at the promise of an emotional connection with you:

- "We bring good things to life."
- "Like a rock."
- "The Big Apple."
- "Have it your way."
- "We are sports."
- "The real thing."
- "We have a gift for giving."
- "Where do you want to go today?"
- "We're all connected."
- "Reach out and touch someone."

All of the companies that created the above slogans did so before extreme competition eroded the ability of products or brands to create these kinds of strong emotional connections. Some of these endure, but the methods to spark the emotional connection may not. That's because nearly every organization has access to the manufacture of outstanding products as well as advertising and the media. Differentiation based on product distinctiveness or the ability to outspend competitors in terms of ad budgets is gone for most organizations embedded within an intensely competitive market. It is therefore increasingly difficult to maintain the sort of brand differentiation that is key to a strong customer relationship. The fixed marketing tools—product, place, price, and promotion—are increasingly even among companies. And while emotional promises still hold real merit, in most cases these long-established marketing tools can't deliver reliably on those promises.

Today the problem advertising faces is that it must meet emotional expectations based on personal contact. In many cases the emotional connection between a brand and a customer ultimately relies on the interaction that the customer has with the people who represent the brand wherever they are—in a store, at a dealership, or on the phone.

A few great organizations know that. That's why they harness the unlimited power of their employees' engagement. That force reaches out to customers who, responding to it on an another level, form long-term relationships with the company through the power of these same employees. These relationships, in turn, are enormously profitable for the organization. Engaged customers spend more, generate higher margins, and become the organization's most passionate advocates.

We derived this information by listening to more than ten million customers over the past decade. Thousands of studies were done. The conclusion was this: Emotion is critical for determining the health of a company's customer relationships.

The difference between merely reaching human senses and engaging human emotions is the difference between generating a transaction and establishing a lasting relationship.

Gallup's studies of customer engagement and retention indicate that customers are not born that way; they stay that way only when they are emotionally engaged.

Engagement derives from the emotional attachment created by outstanding products and brands as well as the powerful interactions of customers' experience with engaged employees.

Here's a sampling.

The Champs and the Chump

Outside the stadium of the team that he supports, Geoff has been waiting patiently for almost an hour, with thousands of other fans, to buy tickets to watch his beloved team compete.

I've been coming to this stadium since I was a kid, with my family and friends. It's historical for me; I grew up here. When I saw legendary hitters launch home runs into the bleachers, I was imprinted for life. It's such an incredible experience to be with the players, the coaches, the manager, and the crowds. As soon as spring training begins I turn to the sports section in the paper first because the anticipation of what is to come is so exciting. I don't care how much tickets cost; they're worth it.

Fans know that great baseball is nothing less than an emotional roller coaster. For fans like Geoff, whose team can't rely on history or high-profile star players to pull fans in, the connection is based on other kinds of emotional engagement.

I've been to other stadiums where I've been appalled at the poorly trained and oblivious counter people and the lack of cleanliness. Here, the organization makes a big effort on behalf of the fans. They send me a yearly Christmas card signed by the players. I get a newsletter in the mail in addition to e-mail updates about the team. I feel that the organization treats me well, that they recognize that the fans pay the players' salaries—and they aren't small. But I never lose sight of how hard these guys play. They represent our city and I'm proud of them.

While Geoff anticipates the game, Igor is standing outside an appliance store. He hopes to get lucky and be one of the hundred fortunate new buyers of an equal number of newly arrived state-of-the-art washing machines. The appliance manufacturer thinks that the perils through which it has to put its advocate customers, who recommend the brand, must stop. So it successfully implements a process reengineering program that results in only a few customers having to wait more than ten minutes in one million possible interactions. In human terms, that means that the organization thinks "zero dissatisfaction" is the ultimate goal. Unfortunately, this myopic viewpoint fails to take into account unanticipated events or problems. Engagement can't be created without human involvement.

A few weeks later Igor decides to buy a refrigerator, so once again, he joins a line to see if he can get the appliance, which boasts a bargain price. This time, however, he is waiting for another brand.

In the meantime Geoff is again standing outside his team's stadium because his team is in the play-offs. This time, he is not only waiting, but also hoping that he can get better seats, which, of course, are more expensive.

Neither Igor nor Geoff minds putting in extra effort. But for the organizations involved, the outcomes are very different. The appliance manufacturer has lost a customer by wrongly assuming that satisfaction with an improved wait-line process would create a return customer. The baseball team, trying hard to please, has engaged fans—because of how they are treated before the team ever wins a game.

Intelligence Gathering at the Supermarket

Both Mrs. White and Mrs. Hunter pride themselves on their radarlike talents for scoping out bargains. When they spotted supermarket sale ads in the local paper, they clipped them and went shopping.

First Mrs. White went to the Food Mart, the source of her ad, and did her weekly shopping here. Then she drove to Shoppers, her regular market, just to compare and see how much she'd saved by buying at the other store.

Mrs. Hunter, however, read the ad from Shoppers, did her shopping there, and then went to Food Mart to do what Mrs. White did.

Interestingly enough, both won the comparison shopping

battle because they purchased different items. But what happens when they need to buy the same items?

Checking out all the different prices in every location is simply unfeasible. Not to mention that the calculations necessary for estimating the possible alternatives to achieve an optimal combination of goods would require the mental capacity of Albert Einstein. In the everyday world of limited information and uncertainty, Mrs. White and Mrs. Hunter resolve their predicament by *asking a next-door neighbor or someone at their supermarket whom they trust what they recommend.*

Despite diverse circumstances, there is a common link between Geoff, Mrs. White, and Mrs. Hunter. All of these engaged customers based their commitment on several factors. Having access to up-to-date information, more adequate knowledge about the options available, and being more certain about the likely benefits of the outcome played a role, but their behavior can be defined by a different motive.

Instead of using clues about better products, improved processes, and reduced prices, they relied on emotionally charged brands and relationships as their incentives for repurchasing in the future:

- Geoff will remain a devout fan of his team as long as the team instills the same pride in him and he feels that they care about him.
- Mrs. Hunter and Mrs. White will keep calling on the advice of people they trust to get the best value for their money.

And what about Igor? Because he responds to lower prices, he will probably spend a lot of time waiting in line for various brands until someone or something makes an emotional connection with him.

Rational versus Emotional:
The "Can't Win" Scenario

Unfortunately, most corporations keep trying to appeal to the rational mind alone instead of to both reason and emotion together. First of all, rationality assumes that behavior is determined exclusively by conscious awareness, reason, and the ability to calculate something's worth. The most recent discoveries in cognitive neuroscience sharply contradict this notion. The research shows that human behavior is influenced by the combination of reason and emotion, and that reason only functions well when it is supported by the presence of an adequate emotional state. So while homing in on conscious awareness and reasoning ability may well work for sparking interest in trying a product (as it did in Igor's case), it fails to produce the emotions required for engagement.

How could it do otherwise, when people with plenty of information at their disposal respond to a product or service by asking themselves, "How did it make me feel?" or "Was I treated special?" or "Were they passionate about solving my needs?" or "Do they specifically know what I like?"

So organizations spend billions of dollars to reach the senses of customers. Flavors delight tongues; the shapes and colors of packages draw eyes; jingles and melodies charm ears; fabrics appeal to touch. All of these strategies, plus product concepts and designs, together with advertising and promotions, target emotions as well as reason. But we know now that the time-honored methods employed to produce those emotions have eroded. Not only that: The emotions required to "try a product" may not be the emotions needed to buy it again.

Organizations suffer the consequences when they adhere to economic principles that dictate that the natural predispositions customers have in relation to products or brands are limited to "more is better than less" or "cheap is better than expensive" or the ever-popular "good is better than bad."

The Revolving Door

One CEO of a Fortune 500 financial organization expressed the concern of many: "Our goal is to reduce—by at least half—the annual rate at which we're losing customers."

Customer retention ranks first among the management concerns of CEOs according to a recent survey by The Conference Board, a widely watched gauge of hot-button issues across a range of industries. It's worth repeating why: The effect of turning even a small proportion of ordinary customers into loyal customers leads to an average increase in profit per customer of more than 25 percent (Frederick F. Reichheld, *The Loyalty Effect*). Although these estimates vary from industry to industry, the point is that in a global market of tight competition, new customers are not enough. Organizations must focus on creating and sustaining loyal customers in order to grow and profit.

Imagine two companies. Company A enjoys a customer retention rate of 80 percent, and company B counts a very respectable rate of 70 percent. Both lose customers every year, but company A is able to keep 10 percent more customers than company B. Let's check out the long-term effect.

Assume that these retention rates hold constant, and that these two companies increase sales by 30 percent each year for a period of ten years. The first year, company A starts with one hundred customers. It loses 20 but acquires 30, so it ends its first year with 110 customers, a 10 percent net increase. Company B, in contrast, starts and ends the year with the same one hundred customers.

In seven years company A will have almost doubled its number of customers, and by the end of a ten-year period it will have seen its customer base grow by a factor of 2.59.

Company B will still have the same one hundred customers. A difference of just 10 percent in customer retention leads these two organizations to dramatically different outcomes.

In most industries the profit earned from each individual customer grows as the customer stays with the company. In some industries the cost of servicing loyal customers even declines as a proportion of operating expenses. So over the course of ten years, company A will have created a positive profit-per-customer effect, driving significant long-term growth and profitability. Company B will have seen the cost of new customers grow as a proportion of earnings, eating away further possibilities for growth and profitability.

For every organization, the accumulation of benefits that follows customer loyalty is crucial. In addition to repeated purchases and higher contributions to profitability, repeat customers engage in various types of behavior that regularly escape the boundaries of current accounting principles. Positive behaviors that increase growth and profitability over time include customer revenue growth, price premiums, account integration, referrals, and tolerance when problems occur. In addition, engaged customers can often cost less to service. It is common knowledge that within very conservative estimates, it costs five times more to attract new customers than to service existing ones.

Corporations have spent billions of dollars trying to attract customers away from competitors. Ever since consumers on market research panels began weighing in on everything from "cereal crunchiness" to "shampoo viscosity," companies have tried to tailor products to meet shoppers' preferences. More recently, as the Internet and other channels became common market research tools, businesses have tracked what individual customers do and don't buy.

With all this information at their fingertips, organizations have now been trying to figure out which business practices make customers faithful.

The Fifth P

Many organizations still try to form the links in the "value chain" in an attempt to forge strong customer relationships. According to the chain ideal, superior competitive advantage can be built from distinct actions. These actions will, it has been believed for decades, differentiate an organization from its competitors while adding superior value to its products and services.

To see if the value chain still holds, Gallup conducted a large study aimed at identifying the relative influence of five key business drivers or marketing tools in creating an intention to repeat purchases in six industries. Included were the traditional four P's of the chain: product, place, promotion, and price. A fifth P—people—representing the interactions between company representatives and customers was added.

Both current and former customers of products and services of those industries were identified, asked about their reactions to the various brands' marketing efforts and service delivery performance, and questioned about their repurchase considerations and plans.

We observed that from the customers' point of view, employees who deal with them not only represent the brand but, in the perceptions of customers, actually *become* the brand.

The fifth P is more effective in differentiating an organization from its competitors than any of the other four P's. Today customers see differences in the quality and capabilities of the people who represent the brands. Here's an example.

Three long-distance phone companies, included in the study, prove the point. The percentages of customers of companies A, B, and C who felt that customer representatives of their carrier were not helpful were, respectively, 6.6, 5.7, and 2.5 times more likely to say that they wouldn't consider their provider in the future. When the quality of technical service was evaluated, customers of companies A and C, who experienced poor service reliability and service in the past, were only 1.9 and 2.4 times more likely to say that they wouldn't consider the carrier in the future. Obviously, a dollar spent improving the relations with customers of either of these companies would be a better investment than a dollar spent improving technical quality.

This same study examined the power of the fifth P among patrons of a fast-food chain. The main reason why both regular and occasional customers return is surprising. It's not the taste of the food. Instead it is the quality of the interactions customers experience with the people who take their orders and serve them. In general, the diners who feel that the staff stand out are roughly five times more likely to return to a specific location. Outstanding advertising can account for only about half of the engagement-building potential of memorably positive personal experiences.

> Engaged customers are worth the time and investment they require because they will repay an emotional recognition of their needs in growth and profits many, many times over.

Will You Love Me Tomorrow?

Yes—and no. First, the bad news: Mounting evidence points out that, in the absence of a meaningful emotional relationship with a brand or an organization, customers are naturally predisposed to switch their allegiance. This means that customers are not born loyal. The good news is that customers are naturally predisposed to be emotionally attached, once emotional connections are established. This information derives from a broad perspective on research findings from numerous clients across a section of worldwide industries. Here's an example, even in an industry where one would assume a human interaction is not needed.

The person in charge of marketing at one of the world's largest soft-drink corporations was interested in finding why consumers returned, so he undertook an in-depth research endeavor. One of the problems he encountered was the misconception that brand managers had about the constancy of their customers. After all, they were used to hearing their brand being referred as the world's greatest soft-drink brand of all time.

Quarter after quarter, managers received dense reports of the market share of their top brand within the soft-drink category. It fluctuated little, hovering at around 50 to 55 percent. The small variation across time periods led to the assumption that these numbers didn't move because purchases were repeated by the same people, that is, dedicated brand drinkers.

But the marketing executive's intuition was not satisfied; he knew that in such a volatile category, there had to be something else happening in the marketplace. He started asking soft-drink buyers about their actual consumption. It turned out that return brand drinkers accounted for only 40 percent of this brand's volume. The other 60 percent came from customers who switched back and forth between brands. (The entire brand measurement and management programs were revamped as a consequence of this unnerving discovery.)

But this marketing executive wasn't satisfied. He asked himself, "Other than flavor, advertising, attractive packaging, and great distribution, what makes people stick to the brand?" This was an insightful question, given that the corporation had always defined its most important marketing goal as "creating the most demand" for its products, and not "creating the highest levels of brand loyalty."

Interestingly, this marketing executive found that conventional wisdom throughout the corporation dictated that repurchase was the result of the brand's "intrinsic and extrinsic benefits" (convenient euphemisms for "product attributes" and "brand image"). He instinctively knew that carbonation, blanket distribution, refrigeration, and great can designs couldn't ensure a customer's return. Finally he made a discovery that may have been worth more than the formula of this company's beverage.

He found that brand image and product characteristics were very strong predictors of product trial, modest predictors of occasional repurchase, but very poor indicators of customer loyalty. But when he asked, "In what types of situations do we find the strongest loyalty to our product and brand?" the answer was both simple and extraordinary.

He found that the heaviest consumption of and strongest fidelity to this brand resulted when people consumed it at home with food in the company of family members and friends.

He also discovered that it was housewives who were the primary purchasers. They bought it repeatedly because of its high emotional connotations: For decades this brand had been overwhelmingly portrayed as the one to be consumed at family gatherings as well as at special occasions (birthdays, New Year's celebrations, parties, and so forth). Another group of repeat buyers were those who liked sharing meals together and felt proud of who they were. In short, he found that dependable consumers of this brand were emotionally attached to it.

In the meantime his corporation was spending billions of dollars worldwide trying to buy allegiance through advertising, proper distribution, and visible refrigeration. But his company was spending hardly any resources in building personal relationships as part of its business model, which survive imitation and price wars.

In the end, this executive discovered that while this product and brand created positive emotions, the model on which the success story had been built had exhausted itself. Traditional marketing, as we know it, had ended. The company now had to think of itself differently (as a total beverage company) and expand its product line with equally exciting brands for all occasions. But more important, the company had to redefine how it created emotional bonds with its customers, and that required incorporating the human-driven aspects of distribution, promotion, sales, and merchandising as part of its engagement model.

This executive learned that even in the beverage industry, where conventional wisdom mandates that emotions are triggered simply by brand advertising, the level of competitiveness now mandates that strong emotional bonds must also be based on human contact. For customer relationships to endure and expand, he learned, they must include positive human interactions. This realization, now embraced by many, has sparked an entire marketing revolution, of which we are witnessing just the beginning.

IT'S ALL IN YOUR HEART

Emotions are the mechanisms that set people's highest-level goals—including what they repurchase. While customers often forget factual information (how much they spent on a service or how much an item costs), they almost always remember their emotions, good and bad—more often the latter than the former—when it comes to deciding whether to buy a product again or keep a service.

This means that the process of deciding whether or not to stay also depends on the emotions experienced while purchasing and using a product or service. So apart from performing its intrinsic functions, a product or a brand carries profound emotional connotations for customers. At the beginning, middle, and end of every transaction, emotional engagement is always at its heart.

There are three kinds of customer loyalty:

- The forced kind, which is imposed by a monopoly and lasts only as long as the monopoly does.
- The bought kind, which is directed at a captive audience (frequent flier coupons are an example, where an airline offers a choice that fliers might not use).
- The emotional kind, which can go on infinitely. Unless you focus on emotional engagement, you will not be able to persuade customers to return to you.

By acknowledging the role emotions play in customer engagement, you have taken the seventh step on The Gallup Path.

CHAPTER 8

The Four Emotional States That Drive Customer Engagement

The Signs Are There

Just as the Q^{12} outlines the environment for employee engagement, the CE^{11}—comprised of the L^3 and A^8—offers concrete ways that organizations can engage their customers.* In order to get to the heart of customer engagement, we studied data stemming from the largest database on the subject. Our work was inspired by some discoveries made by our colleagues William McEwen and John Fleming, who are Gallup's leaders in Customer Engagement Management. We have looked at thousands of questions presented to more than ten million consumers extending over a decade.

First, we reviewed questions about attitudes, opinions, preferences, and behavior that could give clues to the nature of emotional attachment and the characteristics of the special "bond" that links a customer to a company and a brand.

---

*$CE^{11\text{TM}}$, $L^{3\text{TM}}$, and $A^{8\text{TM}}$ are trademarks of The Gallup Organization, Princeton, New Jersey. The CE^{11} items are protected by copyright of The Gallup Organization, 1994–2000. All rights reserved.

In addition, we conducted a second research initiative. It investigated the importance of personal customer–employee relationships as the basis for building brand differentiation and using it as a new source of competitive advantage. This research answered the question: "What are the ingredients for building a strong customer relationship?" The results of these major research undertakings are that:

- The strongest long-term commitment—the emotional allegiance—of a customer to a brand or to an organization does not derive solely from superior factual knowledge and rational appreciation of a product's intrinsic and extrinsic benefits.
- Rather, it is the result of an emotional experience derived from noteworthy interpersonal, product, and brand interactions.

The L^3

Three questions reveal what a customer's attitudes toward engagement really are. They summarize the various rational and emotional considerations in the customer's mind. These questions have been asked by Gallup for years and collectively represent a general measure of "attitudinal loyalty." We call them the L^3 metric.

Question 1: "Overall, how satisfied are you with [brand]?"
Question 2: "How likely are you to continue to choose/repurchase [brand]?"
Question 3: "How likely are you to recommend [brand] to a friend/associate?"

When answering the first question, customers refer to whether or not their past experience met their basic initial expectations—that is, if things went according to plan or if there were problems that were not solved adequately. This question measures whether or not there were any major problems that caused a customer to be dissatisfied.

While bad past experiences are generally more relevant in a customer's mind when considering a repurchase, complete satisfaction does not guarantee repurchase. On the contrary, the analysis conducted by Gallup shows that "complete satisfaction" is merely a predictor of repurchase *consideration*. Rarely is it a sufficient predictor of *actual* purchasing.

The second question measures the customer's intention to return or continue purchasing from the same organization or buy the same brand. It assumes that the customer is thinking about this in reference to past experiences—and perhaps chiefly the most recent one. This question sums up the customer experience and ties it to either a favorable or an unfavorable repercussion in the future. It acts as a concluding foreteller. Intentions, however, are not behavior. Many times customers do not necessarily end up buying what they rationally intended to buy.

The third question addresses word-of-mouth, an inexpensive but critically effective way to expand the usage and value of a branded product or service. The incentive for a customer seeking advice is the reduction in risk associated with the cost of making a wrong decision. It works because the more trusted the person offering it, the more powerful the effect will be. This is why it is so important to see if the customer experience translates into an intention to recommend the experience to others. Recommendations are also important because they set the basic expectations deriving from others about brands, products, or services.

The A^8

The next eight indicators summarize four distinct emotional states, which collectively represent the four basic dimensions of emotional engagement: Confidence, Integrity, Pride, and Passion. As you'll see, each one builds on the one preceding it. One can't be skipped to get to the next level. As with the Q^{12}, the sequence must be followed to work maximally.

CONFIDENCE

> *"[Brand] is a name I can always trust."*
> *"[Brand] always delivers on what they promise."*

Individuals do not automatically trust a brand, product, service, or organization. Neither are they naturally predisposed to think and feel that any of them can be relied upon to consistently deliver the expected or desired outcomes.

Confidence develops out of a "relationship," either through mental images created by brands, through experience with products or services, or by human interactions with employees or representatives. Confidence grows from technical competence, flawless systems, and the proper understanding of all customer needs, including the actions and procedures that must take place. It also depends on the understanding of intangible issues such as treatment and the knowledge required to meet customer expectations.

The key words for trust are "genuine," "authentic," "accurate," and "credible." This emotional bond between an organization or brand and a customer is based on a common understanding of what each expects from the other. More important, it is also the alignment between customer expectations and the actual experience the customer has. Trust speaks of a concept and a promise that are understood and desired. It takes for granted that the organization knows what its customers want, promises to deliver it, and, more important, consistently follows through on that promise.

Meeting these basic expectations, not just once but all the time, builds trust.

The key word relating to promise is "consistency"—that is, knowing that the provider of a service can be trusted to meet expectations on a consistent basis. This in turn speaks of an internal alignment within the organization so that all the processes and systems, including employee interactions with customers, are consistently right.

Destroying Confidence is all too easy. Consider:

- "The other day I went to our usual fast-food place—we usually use the drive-in window—but since one of the kids needed to use the rest room, we went in. The rest rooms were dirty and untidy. This experience was so bad that I will not ever return. I didn't go to this hamburger place because I thought that the rest rooms were clean (I always assumed they were). I went there because the food and the staff were really good. But the rest room experience totally changed my attitude. I just don't have confidence in them any longer."

- "I've been a customer of my bank for years. I always assumed they were good at making sure that all of my balances and statements were accurate. Then one day I noticed on my statement that they had entered the wrong amount (not deliberately, I am sure). But when I looked at that error, it changed my mind about staying with the bank. I felt that they couldn't be relied upon. What if they made a mistake with my retirement fund? I can't trust them."

- The customer of a glass manufacturer whose business was hurt by a late delivery said, "I cannot wait for the time when I will be able to choose another provider and be able to say to these guys, 'I am gone.' I was in charge of a new product line scheduled to hit the store racks in the summer. The product was already stored in refrigerators, the marketing and promotion campaigns were in place—and everything had to be destroyed because this glass manufacturer did not deliver on time. They had promised glass bottles within sixty days, and twice as long went by without delivery seeing a single one. How could I ever rely on them again?"

While Confidence establishes a customer engagement case and helps avoid patron defection, it is not enough to form a complete attachment. When Confidence is firmly established, the first level of emotional bonding is strong enough to support the next levels, starting with Integrity.

INTEGRITY

"[Brand] always treats me fairly."
"If a problem arises, I can always count on [brand] to reach a fair and satisfactory resolution."

Integrity is the belief in a brand's ethical commitment, the unequivocal compliance with principles agreed upon and with a fair resolution of problems or unanticipated events. Integrity is gauged by whether a customer feels fairly treated and by whether she expects a fair resolution to any problems she encounters. That belief is reinforced when a customer feels she is dealing with a company that is not only competent and forthright but also fair and ethical. It can be instilled, for instance, by a salesperson who steers the customer to a product she says she wants instead of immediately pushing the most expensive merchandise. Similarly, if a clerk botches a room reservation, he should know to offer a clear indicator of apology, like an upgrade.

This calls for an organization to define plainly the principles to which it will adhere and the ways in which it will apply these in practical day-to-day scenarios that approach problems from the customer's perspective.

Most organizations write extensive manuals detailing the "what-to-do" in certain circumstances, but a customer's experience is also marked by how these actions were conducted. Therefore, the issues of treatment, employee attitude, and how these actions were implemented, with proper or improper knowledge on the part of the employee, become paramount. The perception that you can depend on an organization to reach a satisfactory problem handling and resolution is the second component of integrity.

The first component of integrity is an adherence to principles that are agreed upon or assumed by both the organization and its customers. It may be the timeline for returning a rebate coupon, a free-trial usage period, a warranty period, or a product return policy.

Some of these principles are formally presented and agreed upon by customers (policies, terms of agreement, and the like), but some other principles are not. These include what a customer and the organization expect to do if an unplanned event unfolds, such as an accident, a computer shutdown, or a natural disaster. Or it may involve a misunderstanding in terms of customer expectations, like a dish at a restaurant that does not look or taste as it was verbally presented by the waiter. A hotel room that does not meet the Internet communication needs of a frequent traveler is another example. It can also mean a piece of apparel that does not suit the person once it is seen at home, or a satellite dish that does not live up to the expectations of signal quality and channel diversity. It takes into account not making a connecting flight due to delays in the incoming flight of the same airline or losing a flight because of airport or other non-airline-related circumstances (weather, increased security, delays). Each of these cases opens up various unplanned scenarios in which customers can—and will—present problems and demand their resolution.

Many unplanned events revolve around solving problems that customers encounter either in the course of using a product or as a result of interacting with the organization's service infrastructure. Sometimes the problem is a need for clear and precise information. Or it can involve the malfunction of a product or the fracture of a service process. Other times it is a complaint. The emotional state that arises as a consequence of this condition is the reassurance that if a problem does arise, the customer can *always* count on the brand, person, or manufacturer to reach a satisfactory resolution.

Here's an example of everything going wrong:

Last year I was relocated to Salt Lake, and (thank the Lord) we were able to quickly find a new home in the process of being built that would meet our moving timelines. The builder was great, and we still were able to add those little special things that would make the house ours. One of the things we wanted was to have the entire house wired for everything technologically possible—computer access in every room, cable/phone in one outlet, surround sound capabilities, security, et cetera. Our builder found a local company specializing in this, and we agreed to pay $8,000 as an add-on for this feature.

When we finally closed and moved in, we called the professionals who had done the wiring for an orientation. An appointment was made for the following Friday at 5:00 P.M. Friday came, and at 4:30 this representative called to tell us that he was going to have to cancel. Well, this was disturbing, as our cable connection seemed random from room to room and our new computer access was inactive. He agreed to reschedule for the following day at 8:30 A.M. The next day, 8:30 rolled around with no sign of him. Finally, almost an hour and a half later, he showed up with three-ring notebooks under both arms, and was ready to help us get going—we thought. Unfortunately, his notebooks were not about how to make this twenty-first-century technology work. They were all about the add-on products we were expected to buy, like infrared security, in-wall speaker system, and modem routers (whatever those are). I quickly stopped him, and kindly told him that we really were not interested in buying add-ons, but were more interested in just getting the basics to work.

His next comment floored me. He let us know that he was in "sales" and not on the "technical service" side, even though he had worked in the service side for the previous five years before his promotion. We pleaded with him to help us with the basics, like watching cable TV and being able to access our Internet provider. He basically said sorry, but we would have to contact technical service and set another appointment. I was livid—and he took offense at my frustration. He picked up his books and informed my wife and me that his organization did not have to do business with our "types." We said, *"Fine!"* But we still needed the spec layout of what wires were where from him. He told us that he would send it out to us the following week. That was five months ago. We have called, e-mailed, and even talked with the senior vice president of service since then. Promises were made with no follow-up. Our builder has tried to resolve this with no luck. I still have $8,000 of high-tech wiring capable of many things, but because of bad follow-through it is sitting useless in my walls.

Sometimes the right actions are taken:

I bought a television that had a $100 rebate. But I had to mail it within thirty days of purchase. I forgot about it, but then I remembered on the last day of the thirty days. So I sent the coupon. I got a letter saying that my application period had expired. Of course, the day when I put the letter in the mailbox we were snowed in, so the post office may have collected it the following day. But when I wrote back explaining the situation, the manufacturer understood my predicament and sent me the rebate. What a nice touch, to be treated fairly.

Here's another example:

I was brought up to believe that using a calculator was high tech. I've always had an internal resistance to dive into the computer era. Obviously, I don't have too much choice; my employer now expects a certain level of competence in their use for communications through e-mail, better presentations, more accurate ability to organize data, and so forth. But when my kids started demanding a home computer—well, to say I was reluctant is an understatement. We did agree that we would look into the possibility (a good way to get them off my back), but then they held me accountable for following through. My thirteen-year-old son brought me a stack of literature on the various options, features, and capabilities. I glanced through it, but felt even more helpless and, frankly, "dumb." But my son recommended that we visit a local supplier to check out the options firsthand.

That is when I met Mark. I hate going to electronics stores because they speak a language that I don't understand. But this guy Mark was different. He seemed to be able to explain things in terms that I could understand, and at the very same time he could address the needs of my son's more sophisticated ear. He was great. There was genuine interest in our needs, and he was very patient with my naïveté. After that first visit, I knew I trusted him, and I took his recommendation.

I feel like the education I got from Mark in those two and a half hours advanced me tenfold in not only understanding this intimidating monster, but also in seeing the possibilities I had before me to be more efficient and productive. Mark not only sold us the computer, but he has personally made himself available for questions as they arose. I've taken him up on that offer many times and so has my son. I will never go to anyone except Mark, even if he changes companies. I guess true loyalty comes out of learning.

When Integrity is firmly established, the two base levels of emotional bonding are strong enough to support the next level, Pride.

PRIDE

> *"I feel proud to be a [brand] customer."*
> *"[Brand] always treats me with respect."*

Engaged customers develop potent feelings that result from the relationship they form with a company through all its touchpoints. These feelings extend well beyond believing that the company keeps its promises and resolves problems. These feelings represent the Pride felt in being associated with a brand and all that it represents.

Brands and organizations establish an engaged relationship with customers when they demonstrate that they support and reinforce the customers' emotions of self-worth.

The key words here are "dignity," "deference," "kindness," and "courtesy." They reflect an organization that acknowledges and values a customer as more than a number. Respect is conveyed when brands, products, and organizations clearly recognize the human value of their customers and show that they hold them in high esteem.

No matter how strong the emotional connection is on the other two levels, pride can be lost if the company fails to demonstrate respect for the customer:

As CFO, my responsibilities span a wide arena. But my most important mission is the accurate organization of financial data reflecting this company's fiscal progress or lack thereof. We have all the latest technology, and some of the best people I have ever worked with on my accounting team. But who holds accounting account-able? It is really the third-party audit firm we use to re-view our work each year. Many times I hear other CFOs complain about this process and how much of a pain it is. But I guess I am the opposite; I welcome this year-end flurry because my relationship isn't with the "firm." It's with Norm. Norm and I have worked together for four years, and he has come to know our organization, our business strategies, and me very well. He isn't the tradi-tional count, observe, and report kind of guy. He always sees an opportunity or direction in the numbers.

Sometimes I get so close to it all, I miss some really important stuff. He doesn't and so he is my insurance of not missing something critical. It isn't always comfort-able working with Norm, though, because he isn't afraid to challenge and then stand firm until I break out of my insulated point of view. He keeps an eye on the present state, but never lets us stop seeing the future and longer-term issues to come. Norm has become a real trusted friend. We have lunch once a month, we talk fre-quently by phone, and he is the first I call when a trou-bling issue is hitting me in the face. I know that we are required to use one of the major firms, but I sure hope they know my loyalty is to Norm, and thus to the firm. Not the other way around.

If pride and respect are demonstrated, the customer may reward the company with the very highest level of emotional bonding to a brand: the feeling of Passion.

PASSION

"[Brand] is the perfect company for people like me."
"I can't imagine a world without [brand]."

When a customer refuses to accept an equally attractive substitute for a product and says, "No thanks. I'll wait for what I want even if I have to pay more for it," her Passion is showing.

When a consumer drives longer to buy a specific brand of motor oil and absolutely refuses to accept anything else, his Passion is obvious. The same is true for people who line up for long waits in the midsummer heat just to see the smiles on their children's faces at their preferred theme park. When a Passionate connection is present, nothing can replace it.

Passion cannot be established in the heart and mind of a customer unless the three previous emotional levels are in place. Perfect alignment of expectations and consistency in every customer interaction—with products, services, systems, processes, and people—must be established.

At this stage of the relationship, cost takes on a much less important role. Customers who feel Passion for a brand or an organization often express the sentiment, "I cannot imagine a world without it." If they are deprived of a specific brand, product, or service, they can actually suffer from withdrawal.

I just couldn't believe it when an old, venerable chain store closed a couple of years ago. It was always there; my grandmother talked about shopping there. I practically grew up in one. There were toys and makeup and then inexpensive housewares. There was so much variety, and the prices were great. And the convenience—I could buy potting soil and picture frames at the same time. I still miss it. I know nothing will ever replace it.

The great organizations know how to build and keep Passion:

I love to shop in this place. They have the things I like and good prices, but most importantly, they treat me like no other place—that is, with regard and kindness. And that creates the right atmosphere for me. They don't show a bad attitude if I don't like something, or if I end up not buying that day. They are there for me, helping me find the stuff I like, and they show enormous respect for the customer, for people like me, for everyone.

IT ALL ADDS UP

The emotional indicators of the CE^{11} add up to this unwavering point: You can't maximize your profit unless you create Passion. That means letting go of all the old, tired, etched-in-stone "rules" you have used in the past to determine customer "loyalty." Customers are emotional beings who respond in their own ways. You can't buy their engagement—but you can make it happen.

The CE^{11} is the customer engagement metric to use to measure the "attitudinal loyalty" and emotional connection of your customers. It does so by pinpointing the emotional factors that determine whether or not they will return to you:

- Overall satisfaction.
- Intention to repurchase.

- Intention to recommend a brand, product, or service.

   It also measure four basic emotional states:

- Confidence: the knowledge that promises will be kept.
- Integrity: fair treatment when problems arise.
- Pride: respect for customers while supporting their self-worth.
- Passion: the irreplaceable connection and a perfect personal "fit" between a company and a customer.

By understanding the eleven indicators of customer engagement and how they will impact on your brand, product, or organization, you have taken the eighth step on The Gallup Path.

CHAPTER 9

Directions for Enhancing and Managing Customer Engagement

Let Me Get That for You

Running a successful restaurant depends on a lot of things: location, a good chef, an efficient waitstaff, fresh ingredients, a pleasant atmosphere, attractive table-ware, flattering lighting; the list goes on and on. But you can have all these things and fail if your customers don't keep coming back.

So states Steve, a manager who has been responsible for transforming three restaurants into the top places to dine over a twenty-year period.

I never "assume" that customers will come back. I try to appeal to them in a personal way, because experience has shown me, over and over again, that it's the only system that works.

As the manager, he is the go-between linking the employees and all of their many functions with the customers who walk in—and out—the doors every day. Like other great managers, he relies on an unbeatable combination of three actions.

First, he knows the specific talent themes of every employee. By taking the time to find these out, he can direct their strengths in the most effective directions. For instance, no one knows, or describes the desserts better, than the pastry chef at one of his restaurants. So whenever a customer hesitates, the pastry chef, who is a gifted communicator, sprints out of the kitchen for a quick consultation. It's a rare night when a diner passes on one of his labors of love and sugar. From that point on, a lot of customers ask for a personal "dessert consultation." The pastry chef knows the likes and dislikes of regular customers and, for special occasions, like a birthday or anniversary, will prepare something just for them.

Second, he meets the expectations of his customers every time they arrive. That means the way he runs the restaurants, the treatment people receive, and the advice they hear about food and wine selections is consistent. Where the advice is concerned, he takes it one step farther. He's up front, which translates into honesty of the waitstaff when asked about a certain dish or bottle of wine.

Third, Steve knows the likes and dislikes of his regular patrons. Because of this, he is able to initiate something new with all repeat customers each time they come in. While this isn't the easiest thing to do, he realizes that it's imperative if he wants to keep his customer relationships strong. One day he will offer an unusual dessert or an innovative tasting plate of appetizers. Sometimes he will initiate a conversation about a new bottle of wine that he just stocked. Some nights he'll talk about the seasonal flower arrangements, and how he first saw a particular blossom on a trip abroad. Because he is so tuned in to what his customers like and dislike, he remembers what regular patrons prefer to drink and brings them filled glasses as soon as they are seated. He knows whether they are usually in a rush or whether they prefer to linger. In sync with their food preferences, he'll make a recommendation based on their personal tastes. And when a celebration is in full swing, he'll stop by and chat for a bit, just as a friend would.

With a trio of thriving restaurants in a highly competitive market, Steve bases his continued success on establishing—and maintaining—a deep connection with every patron. That, he knows, is the way to keep his restaurants full.

Steve's actions mirror those of countless great managers to establish an emotional link with customers.

The Three Links

No matter where they take place or what kind of brand, product, or organization they involve, every employee–customer interaction involves three simultaneous processes: actions, treatment, and knowledge.

- **Actions** are the functional aspects—that is, all the activities that an employee is supposed to perform on the customer's behalf. For instance, when a passenger checks in at a hotel, this includes transforming a reservation into a registration, taking note of the guest's information, asking for preferences, and delivering information.
- **Treatment** represents the employee's personal touch, the positive or negative attitudes that set the tone of the customer's emotional response to what the employee is doing. Friendliness, courtesy, and respect represent frequently mentioned characteristics of personal treatment.
- **Knowledge** refers to information and advice, which customers appreciate as "enhancing the value" of their experience. Factual information is the component that usually becomes the center of attention from a functional perspective. Advice, however, can only be valuable as a result of the

interpretation of information filtered through the talent themes of an employee.

The important thing to remember is this: While the action component is driven by the organization's functional structure, treatment and knowledge are not. These two are dependent upon the particular innate inclinations of every individual in a team. These traits cannot always be passed along from person to person, cannot always be scripted or systematized. That's why being aware of the individual personal strengths of every front-line employee is so crucial. Developing the awareness about how each of these strengths can be productively applied to enhance the customer experience, thereby promoting emotional attachment, is the key component of a manager's job.

The process breaks down this way. Actions, along with a fraction of knowledge, are processed by the rational mind. However, the rest of the process—the majority of the knowledge and all of the treatment—are stored as emotional memory. These aspects are "felt."

There are as many variations on fitting the expectations of an engaging customer relationship as there are stars in the universe. In some situations the customer touchpoint is fast paced, allowing just a few seconds for personal impact. What occurs in the first seven seconds of the interaction between a person selling cars and a customer buying one sets the emotional stage for the entire proceedings.

In others the interaction is continuous, requiring very different employee strength applications. In the case of a financial adviser, the needs of a customer may go on for years, so success might be measured in paying attention to the client's comfort zone, and knowing when to suggest an investment and when to pull back.

No employee can be scripted to generate the right emotions in others. Nor can the emotional mind be fooled. It senses whether an interaction is genuinely positive or negative. That's why the great managers use three links, to make sure that action, treatment, and knowledge are achieved every time an employee interacts with a customer.

First Link: Align Employee Strengths to Meet Customer Expectations

Great managers recognize that every employee has talent themes and possesses a unique style of building and cultivating strong personal relationships. So the manager's first step is gaining awareness of individual talent themes that can evoke a positive emotional state in the customer.

The second step is to position these talent themes to effectively promote emotional attachment.

For example, to Karina, a fund-raiser who works for a midwestern university, there are no strangers. She likes meeting new people all the time and feels passionate about the significance of what her organization does. Her natural predispositions allow her to excel at greeting visitors and making them feel welcome and confident about the goals of the organization. Through her work, she maintains an astounding thousand-plus relationships with potential patrons of the university. She accounts for the impressive number this way: "I guess my excitement transfers to new contributors and they want to be a part of the future of what I see as an incredible university." That's why Karina has been placed where she is by a savvy supervisor.

The manager of a large metropolitan florist said:

Our floral business addresses all kinds of needs. Certainly our customers rely on us to give them what they want. However, while our flower arrangers know how to create stunning arrangements, some possess a magic touch when it comes to pleasing our customers. They understand the emotional side of flowers: what they mean when they are given and received, what they represent at celebrations or funerals. They convey that feeling to customers, who always respond favorably to them. A comfort level is formed between them, which opens up a whole other world of types of flowers to use, numbers of arrangements to buy, planning for the future—the list goes on and on.

Second Link: Initiate, Sustain, and Restore Customer Emotional States

Great managers of customer engagement always regard customers as individuals waiting for an emotional state to be initiated, sustained, or restored.

The second link is very often a team effort. This means that a manager must make sure that the customer feels the combined effort of everyone involved. He figures out how the specific talent themes of employees will affect every growth strategy of the organization. That means sales, service, product quality, innovation, support, and marketing.

I thought that buying a new stereo system would be an exercise in frustration, because when I purchased my first one I felt like an idiot. More to the point, I was helped to feel like an idiot by the salesperson, who regarded me that way.

This time, however, when I went to a different store, I was amazed. Not only was I greeted at the door and asked if I could be helped and then directed by a very pleasant woman, [but] Mike, the salesperson who helped me, didn't push the most expensive sound system on me. Instead, he asked about the size of the room I wanted the system for, what I presently had, and why I wanted to replace it. He spent a lot of time with me, showed me how to use the different equipment—which was a relief because I'm also concerned that either I'll break something or mess it up so badly I won't ever be able to use it. He answered every one of my questions patiently and reassured me that I was not alone in feeling overwhelmed by the ever-changing technology. Even the checkout person made be feel good. What a relief.

Third Link: Intensify the Consistency of Emotional States

Often emotional states are affected by what goes on at a different branch of a business because of the actions of other employees or teams. Great organizations realize this—it's why they embark on companywide efforts to consolidate and intensify consistency. It's why they measure the emotional states of customers on an ongoing basis, and why they hold every single team and employee accountable for the emotional impact they have on the customer. It's also why they review, on a regular basis, the consistency of customer engagement among and within teams. The customers' experience needs to be unique and consistent across all points and all moments that you "touch" the customer. The best organizations create a culture around serving the customer that is so consistent and passionate that no one individual or team has a choice but to join the continuous effort of engaging the customer, one at a time.

One company accomplished high levels of customer focus by literally exposing every associate to the customer and his needs. Whether you work in operations, accounting, or human resources, you will see, listen to, and talk with a customer and be exposed to their needs and lives. In this industry, like many, only sales and service representatives are supposed to interact with the customer. But in this company everyone is customer facing, regardless of their role.

Most organizations have little alignment, focus, or accountability as it comes to the emotional engagement of their customers.

> My daughter is ten years old, and we adopted her at birth. One of the things we agreed to up front with her natural mother was to remain in contact and to share pictures, birthday and Christmas gifts, and so forth. Three Christmases ago, my daughter received a dress from her birth mother. Unfortunately, it was the wrong size. With the gift was a letter telling me where she got it (a national chain with many stores) and if there was a size problem, it could be exchanged. Well, I took the dress to my local store, and was told that it could only be exchanged at the place of purchase. I explained in detail the situation, and was basically told that rules are rules.
>
> I then called the original store and was greeted by a very pleasant young woman, who quickly understood the situation, and asked me to send it back for another size. I did just that. Two weeks later I received the package back just as I had sent it, explaining that there was no receipt, and thus no exchange was possible. I then quickly called the store again, and was told by a supervisor that this was policy; I was basically out of luck with no receipt. I was shocked. I had done business with my local store for years, and had been very satisfied. This was too much. It breaks my heart every time I think about this, as my daughter really was hurt and disappointed. This chain has recently filed for bankruptcy; I can see why, and I could have told them where they were headed two years ago.

In addition to using the three links to keep their employees and customers emotionally engaged, great managers, and the organizations they work for, do something else. They know when to let a customer go.

Not All Customers Are Created Equal

The notion that "all customers count the same" is as wrong as the idea that "all employees can excel at anything provided that they try hard enough."

Great organizations know that their best customers are those who respond in kind to the interaction with engaged employees. But they are equally good at identifying the worst customers.

Said a frequent business traveler:

I'm a top-award client of all the major hotel chains, and what I care about are discounts. As soon as I check into my room I start looking for things that don't work or are missing. I complain about service. That way I get the price of the room down. It's gotten to the point where the front-desk employees know me—and try to avoid me.

With good reason. These put-upon employees feel threatened by the very real possibility that the traveler will register a complaint about them with the manager. Every time this person shows up he depresses the engagement of the employees with whom he comes into contact.

Is he worth the aggravation?

On the other hand, there are guests who routinely book very expensive suites and never ask for a discount. At the same time they are sensitive to and appreciative of the attention they receive at the hotels. As a consequence, the engagement level on both sides keeps being reinforced.

Fire the Bad Customer: It Makes Good Sense

It may seem akin to blasphemy to say so, but great organizations know that before they let employees go, they should consider letting customers go instead. This is not a spur-of-the-moment decision. Rather, it's one based on just what the customer does or doesn't bring to the relationship. Customers who are constantly demanding, who complain no matter the extent of the effort made on their behalf, or who won't try to seek a common ground with employees are a continual drain on employees. When mutual respect isn't present, and cannot be created, the value of the customer dissipates. Are customers like these worth the effort that so many people must make on their behalf?

Recalled the CEO of a large and very successful consulting organization:

> A few years ago, as our profits declined slightly, my executive committee started debating about whether or not a reduced employee base would be a good idea to boost profits. I knew that the majority of my employees were talented and engaged. There was also a proportion of employees who were talented but not engaged. The reason was that they were servicing accounts that just valued low prices. I looked at the profit margins of these accounts and quickly discovered that they were actually costing more than what these clients paid. Then I added the hidden cost of not fully engaged employees. So I considered an alternative solution to fix the profitability problem. I decided to fire the bad customers instead of letting go of good employees. The idea paid off, too. My organization's profits rose considerably.

Terminating actively disengaged customers is not only a personal issue; it affects business as well. Consider this example. When a medium-sized consulting organization saw its profits decline to 2 percent in one year as a consequence of what was defined at the time as "bad customer relationships," it decided to terminate those accounts. The "bad customers" were a major proportion of this organization's business—a full 15 percent. In total, they represented $40 million in lost revenue. Nonetheless, the accounts were terminated. One year later the pruning of these accounts contributed to an increase in profitability to 8 percent (a full 6 percent increase) and a reduction in employee turnover of approximately 3 percent.

Bad Customer Symptoms: Six Warning Signs

Bad customers are costly, not only in terms of the additional—and sometimes limitless—resources they demand, but also in terms of the effect they have on the emotional states of your organization's employees and their level of engagement.

These are six signs that great managers look for to diagnose the health of the organization's customer relationships. If they are present, great managers act like doctors. They try to treat the problem—and sometimes they cut the bad customers out.

SYMPTOM 1: EMPLOYEE BURNOUT

When the most engaged employee runs away from a client, it's a sure sign that this customer is trouble. Bad treatment—including abuse—suffered when dealing with an actively disengaged customer is not something that employees should be subjected to.

As a nursing director, my ultimate goal is the wellness and healing of my patients. Our nursing staff is the conduit to that end. A couple of years ago, we had a very demanding physician, which was fine, but his approach to our nurses was unforgivable. Virtually every nurse throughout the hospital would do everything in their power to avoid his berating and demeaning treatment of them. No one would work with him as he ascended upon the floors. He would literally reduce associates to tears with his personal attacks upon them. The fact that there was no reason for the attacks was brought to his attention on many occasions by our administration, but he refused to see his role in this unfortunate crisis, and did nothing to either take responsibility or make changes. This inappropriate treatment of our staff carried over to his patients, and literally eroded any patient faithfulness and staff morale. We only have nineteen physicians in this community, and the next nearest hospital is sixty-nine miles away. We felt stuck.

Finally we were forced to discontinue his privileges at our facility. Fearing complaints and backlash from other physicians and patients, we actually were surprised to find the opposite. By taking this action, we actually set boundaries and were able to act on our values, versus just state them. The support for this action was widespread, and we received hundreds of comments about our courage and willingness to stand up for our people, and the integrity that demonstrated.

SYMPTOM 2: THE PROBLEM ZONE

The second sign of a customer or an account that may be a candidate for termination involves consistently negative attitudes on the part of a client. A problem or an unanticipated event may have occurred that initially created a negative emotional state in the customer. But in attempt after attempt to restore this emotional state, the client chooses to remain in the "problem zone." No matter how much the organization tries, or how many resources it allocates to please the customer, she just does not budge. This is a sign that the relationship may benefit from the parties parting ways.

I started a small advertising and promotions agency in the 1980s and have developed quite a niche for very specialized work within the health care arena. We have eighteen associates, and I would put their creative talent themes and customer service up against any Chicago or New York agency. We keep clients; we've rarely lost one. But about once a year, we will win the business for a new account, begin work on helping them extend their mission, and sometimes realize that we and the client don't have the right chemistry. Usually I notice this very quickly, and sometimes ignore or minimize the arising conflicts. But the worst are those cases where we try to build a partnership and the client will not allow it to happen. Inevitably, problems arise (as they always do in the creative process), and the client contact becomes livid. My true test for knowing when to move on is when the client will not even attempt to enter into the solution phase of an issue, and continually almost fights to keep the crisis fires burning. Hey, I'm a businesswoman, and I realize problems happen, but when you can't get past it, it's time to move on and apply your energies elsewhere. I just wish sometimes that I could muster up the courage to act sooner. It would sure be better for me, my associates, and our image.

SYMPTOM 3: NO RESPECT

A third sign of a bad customer involves a clear and evident crack in the foundation of mutual respect. As the organization's employees and the client tackle the resolution of a problem, or as the employee–customer interactions unfold, the customer may have lost respect for the organization or the individual employees servicing the account. A possible conflict becomes instead a "personal issue" to the customer. Without respect for the organization or its employees, there cannot be a real opportunity for a sustained partnership.

> In banking we deal with very personal issues and special individual needs of customers. Our branch knows all of our customers very well, and I really mean all of them. What many don't understand is that to have a good service orientation and culture, you also need to make some tough decisions. Four years ago I had to make one of those decisions. We had a very important ($$) customer, who would continually cause difficulties upon her arrival at the branch. She would literally scream at people who were doing everything in their power to help her. One month I counted these outbursts; they totaled sixteen.
>
> We tried everything, starting with the personal banker approach, and she literally demanded the firing of every one of the six personal bankers she dealt with. Finally, after realizing that we had exhausted every possible solution, we requested a meeting with this customer, which included myself as the branch manager and our branch senior vice president. We took the approach that obviously we were not meeting her needs, and really were sincerely committed to helping her find another banking institution that would. She was shocked at our proposal. She had no idea we were perplexed with her obvious dissatisfaction. She even went

so far as to say, "I am not dissatisfied!" When we reviewed some of the specific situations with her, she became visibly embarrassed, and softened before our very eyes. She requested to not be transferred to another institution and even suggested that she reunite with the second personal banker she had dealt with. We then asked that banker into the meeting, and new ground rules were laid and boundaries became clear. This customer has become a very solid member of our banking group. It is amazing what happens when respect reenters a relationship.

SYMPTOM 4: OBSTACLES TO EFFECTIVENESS

This may include blocking access to indispensable resources, withholding information vital to the effective functioning of the product or service, blocking of access to individuals involved in the reception or delivery process, or resistance to taking the appropriate actions to operate or service the product.

As a health and benefits consultant to many large organizations, I encounter many human resource professionals. They are day-to-day customers, but I always try to keep the perspective that every employee and their respective family members are my real customers. Anyway, I have really struggled with those daily contacts that pigeonhole me, and virtually rope me off from any other relationships in the organization. My clients pay me a lot of money to keep up to date and in touch with the latest employee benefit offerings. What is sad is that one person (my HR contact) makes all the decisions when it comes to my recommendations. I am literally never able to present these ideas to others when in fact, I am then held accountable for the effectiveness or lack

thereof of the programs this one person "lets through."
I have too much of a belief in the power of what we
bring to employees to just let this go on. When this happens, I resign my services. Now this tends to go one of
two ways: (a) I am told to not let the door hit me in the
face, or (b) I get the attention of senior decision makers.
Either way is better than what it was, and I feel like I
am actively representing my real customers. I also can
sleep well at night knowing that my clients are fully
aware and using the best possible benefit programs
available.

SYMPTOM 5: A RELATIONSHIP BASED SOLELY ON PRICE

When the only basis for a business relationship is an exclusive focus on lower prices, trouble will follow. In practice,
this sign takes many possible expressions, from the usual "If
you don't match the price of your competitor, I will discontinue being your customer" to the more subtle "Next time it
will have to be cheaper or else I will not come back."

> After I saw a lot of ads from a telecommunications con-
> glomerate stating that the only difference between them
> and all the other carriers was price, I figured that I was
> one lucky customer. I get calls all the time, along with
> pieces in the mail from various suppliers, offering me
> lower rates. So I keep changing carriers. They keep giv-
> ing me extras like more long-distance minutes or air-
> lines miles or other perks. No one seems to care; no one
> follows up. As long as the prices keep dropping, I'm
> going to keep on moving from carrier to carrier.

SYMPTOM 6: TAKING THE RELATIONSHIP FOR GRANTED

So much emphasis is placed on products and processes within organizations that often the customer relationship factor goes unaccounted for. How much do such organizations value the quality of the relationships they have with their customers? Unfortunately, very little. In the best-case scenarios organizations take the value of these relationships for granted, as a nondifferentiated and relatively weak factor affecting their business. "No news is always good news" seems to be the regular assumption.

> I oversee the consulting practice within our organization. I have a lot of contact with our clients. Occasionally I get called upon to solve a crisis or problem that has come up with one of our engagements. I always approach this swiftly, but also very carefully. Emotions are always involved, and I try to collect all the facts I can before intervening with a specific plan of action. A couple of years ago a problem erupted. I set forth on my fact-finding expedition and truly was confused to find that the problem areas pointed out by the client were not founded. Now, don't get me wrong; this is not a case of "ignore the problem" or "find someone to blame as a defense mechanism." These issues were seemingly being blown out of proportion, and frankly the associates involved were feeling as helpless as I in not knowing what to do.
>
> I spent literally hours on the phone, carefully detailing the misgivings that they were upset about. I then tried the best I could to develop an actual process redesign to better meet the needs of this client. Hours of attention went toward this, and I was impressed with the layout. When the morning came to present this to the unhappy client, I handed out this document for review and presentation. Immediately this client began to

thumb through the plan, and stopped me in my tracks with the comment, "There is a typo on page thirteen." Embarrassed and humbled, I proceeded with the presentation. But no matter what was presented, she was unable to get past that typo on page thirteen, and kept using this as a point of reference as to why the general displeasure occurred in the first place. I offered to reprint the entire document, but she relented, stating that she was going to use this as the main example of the subpar work she had been seeing.

Finally I came to the point of closing my presentation and stating that it may be time to get honest with each other and admit that we didn't match up very well. This statement caused a surprise reaction. She immediately took a "how dare you" position, but I calmly restated my decision. As if a ten-thousand-volt shock hit her, she realized that I was serious. Not knowing what to say, she became overcome with uncertainty as to what to do. She then immediately did an about-face. She seemed to realize for the first time that she needed us as badly as we needed her for this engagement to be successful. A different willingness appeared in the relationship, and I am surprised to report that our account with this organization has tripled since then. I don't always like to be the bad guy, but sometimes representing yourself also means standing up for yourself. In this case respect and partnership were reborn.

Management 101

A customer service representative told us:

I always look at problems as an opportunity that we have to make our customers find that we are really good at what we do, and that includes living up to our commitments. Handling a problem or something that comes up unexpectedly is an opportunity because if there weren't problems or things like these, our customers would never know that we are different; we are special. A problem is not something to be minimized. It is an opportunity to make our customers feel that they are treated fairly.

Great managers understand that without the best action, treatment, and knowledge on behalf of employees, it is virtually impossible to build the four levels of customer engagement: Confidence, Integrity, Pride, and Passion.

Great managers make sure that the emotional indicators of the CE[11] are met in order to ensure continued growth and profits. Here's how they do it.

BUILD CONFIDENCE

Requirement: Clarify the brand promise and deliver on that promise every time.

Most organizations mistakenly assume that quality products and efficient systems deliver confidence. Great managers ensure that their employees inspire confidence.

In quality assurance, for instance, employees with a natural predisposition for perfection and follow-through, laser-like focus, and unbending commitment will probably do well. These strengths are clearly related to the outcome of confidence in a product or service.

BUILD INTEGRITY

Requirement: Proper handling of unusual or problematic situations.

Employees who are passionate about solving problems, maintain control when challenged, and yet remain very positive and helpful possess many theme combinations that make them ideal candidates to be in charge of facing and fixing knotty problems, either by themselves or within a team. Those who naturally seek to create and maintain a pleasurable and consistent experience for customers do so because it is who they are. They are the ultimate "hosts." These employees believe that people function best in a consistent and comfortable environment, where the rules are clear and are applied to everyone equally. Being treated this way can provide an enormous emotional boost to a customer, who will not forget it.

For customers, this means that their needs are viewed as important, which reflects on their own value.

BUILD PRIDE

Requirements: Unique experiences that enhance a customer's esteem.

Some employees possess the natural gift of a self-perceived level of excellence. Employees yearning to be admired as credible professionals and successful individuals carry that passion to work and aim it at impacting others. That aim transfers to customers, who respond by wanting to be part of a winning team, too. Additionally, customers feel respected, because the genuine feelings of employees toward them help them realize their worth. If you want your customers to feel respected, let them interact with employees who care.

BUILD PASSION

Requirement: One-on-one relationships.

Some employees are naturally drawn to the distinctive needs and interests of each customer. To them, references such as "these are the customers' requirements" are mere generalizations. This gift taps into the ability to see the unique characteristics of each person they come into contact with. It represents a very powerful force that can be applied to complete the cycle of engagement, especially when it is combined with and complemented by the other employee strengths. The manufacturer of a prestigious sports car, for instance, discovered that its customers were especially proud of technical aspects of the car's design and performance. In response, it successfully selected and positioned employees with the strong natural desire to know more, and who felt confident and truly energized in their discussions with these sophisticated car owners/buyers.

Some individuals exhibit a superior ability to develop a vision of what the future holds in terms of possible new uses of current and new products and services. These people and teams are always looking forward and asking "what if?"

Other teams are capable of making a more powerful use of their engaging resources through their ability to "sort through the clutter" and set a direction, and then follow through on it. "Well planned and well managed" is the mantra of this group.

Still others are capable of producing greater results by virtue of an intense never-ending need to keep progressing, improving, and moving forward.

When everything is in place, customers return. Here's what the CEO of a large upscale department store had to say about the CE[11]:

My customers keep coming back because of a purchasing experience they like to feel and repeat over and over again. To some extent, it's the image of themselves that they will project through a brand or a product, but they only get to see that image when they feel a certain atmosphere. The tangibles that are employed to create this atmosphere are important. We need a nice floor with flowers, lights and lots of adornments, but as important (if not more important) are the employee-related attitudes and behavior that create this atmosphere in the customers' memory: how they are treated, how our employees facilitate their purchase experience and make it pleasurable. My best employees always start and stop from only that perspective.

The CEO of one of the seven largest U.S. banks concurred:

Whenever a customer has an interaction with an employee, he or she emerges more or less engaged to our company and never stays the same as before. The issue of engaging customers is not one dictated by the types of employees that they deal with every time they interact with our company. All employees carry virtually the same weight, all the way from the security guard to the officer of the bank. Each can and will affect the emotional experience of a customer. In the end, they all count the same.

DO WHAT THE GREAT MANAGERS DO

There's no other way around it, through it, or under it. If you want to be part of a great organization, you have to ensure that your customers keep coming back because they respond to your emotionally engaged employees. Achieving this goal means using a direct approach that works. Isn't it time that you use the same method, too?

Do what the great managers do, and engage your customers by:

- Identifying and using employee talent themes so that they generate emotional engagement by doing what they do best.
- Initiating, sustaining, or restoring their emotional states.
- Intensifying emotional states by making sure that employee–customer engagement is consistent.

By accepting what managing to enhance and sustain customer engagement means, you have taken the ninth step on The Gallup Path.

Emotional Economics, Part 2

The Engagement Profits

Just as the Q^{12} indicates growth and profit where employees are concerned, the CE^{11} specifies growth and profit where customers are concerned. It does so for a fundamental reason: *Customer engagement directly predicts repurchase and the likelihood of a continuing customer relationship.*

But just as there is more than one kind of employee engagement, customer engagement is not one-of-a-kind. The data we assembled explored the combination of scores across the eleven measures of customer engagement, which, in turn, define four distinct customer groups. These are mutually exclusive customer segments established through specific engagement items that represent a substantial impact on business outcomes.

To clarify these levels of engagement groupings, Gallup concluded that customers belong to one of four relevant groups. In terms of their level of engagement, customers may either be fully engaged, engaged, not-engaged, or actively disengaged.

Using these categories it is, finally, possible to measure the effect of customer relationships—positive or negative—on organizational business outcomes. Not only do these four groups differ in terms of revealing the overall presence or relative absence of engagement, but their various sizes and proportions reflect a wide range of engagement performance within an organization as well.

This metric was developed so that organizations could use it to gauge the revenue growth potential among their *existing* customers. Consequently, this provides a considerable shift in strategic vision: The most direct route to sustainable growth and profitability for most companies is not through new customers but through a current customer base. But while some customers are already at the top levels of engagement, the majority of the customer base is still waiting to experience full engagement.

Understanding where your customers stand in the group, and helping them find their way to being the fully engaged people they long to be, is the way to real profit and growth.

The Fully Engaged

I thought that buying things was something that we just had to do, something to satisfy our basic needs. But in the course of getting to know your products and being in contact with your organization I have learned that I can enjoy being your customer. You have made me feel important and valuable; I can always count on you. I often ask myself this question: "Why didn't I contact you before?" You are not only the best there is—the way you make me feel as a customer is truly legendary.

Explained the manager of a large call center facility:

The time came when we had to review our telephone service contract. The problem was that our current supplier came with a proposal that was $400,000 more expensive than that of their main competitor. This competitor actually came to me and said, "We want to make a formal promise that we will lower the price of your current supplier no matter what the price they finally present to you." It was a very difficult decision at the onset. When I asked my team their opinion they said they wanted to stay with our current supplier. There was no way of making them look at the possibility of another one. They came up with great reasons. They said that the advice they got from our current supplier was simply invaluable, as was their reaction whenever we had problems. Then there was the very strong commitment with every aspect of our business. In the end, they won. We are paying a lot more for those "intangibles" but we all think that it is worth it. Somehow, these guys have found a way to enter the emotional heart of my organization.

These are the words of fully engaged customers.

Most businesses count on a small proportion of such people. They represent an organization's most treasured resource because of their strong attachment to that organization.

The fully engaged customer profile:

- Responsive: They pay their bills promptly.
- Positive: They show a consistent pattern of effective use of the organization's service infrastructure because they learn about the organization and are willing to try new products and services.
- Listeners: They are most likely to welcome the organization's innovations and try new products or brand extensions.
- Fair: They are least likely to submit unreasonable restitution claims.

- Sustainable: They value long-term relationships with their brands and provider organizations.

These wonderful customers account for more than just sales and increased cash flow. They cost less to manage, become strong brand advocates, represent higher profits, and become the most reliable source of sustainable growth and profitability.

The Engaged

I've flown with you a hundred times in the last year. I'm supposed to be a Gold Card member with you and yet I ask myself this question: "Did you see how badly the check-in clerk treated me?" Actually I don't think she discriminates among passengers. She just treats everyone equally badly.

These are the words of an engaged passenger but certainly not a fully engaged one. These engaged customers are attached by positive emotional connections—but at levels markedly less strong than of those who are fully engaged. Their positive emotions about a brand or an organization are insufficient to result in a strong commitment to buy that product or service again. They may be attitudinally loyal, but are not emotionally attached. These are good customers who perceive an enhanced level of value in an organization's service infrastructure. However, they may also harbor doubts as to benefits that are supposedly exclusive to what the organization is offering. They represent a reservoir of potential.

The engaged customer profile:

- Collectively represent 20 to 25 percent of a company's customers. This group also includes customers who contribute a lot of their business but have not allocated the greatest proportion of their business to a single organization.

- Sensitive to improvements in products as well as pricing policies.
- Represent primary targets for products and may expand into additional services if a stronger emotional bond is forged.

The Not-Engaged

It doesn't matter to me where I go to buy what I need, as long as the price is good and the place is nearby. I pride myself on being a good shopper and searching out bargains. Every store has them; it's just a matter of finding them. When I do, I get a whole lot of satisfaction. As far as sticking with one store goes, why should I?

These are the words of a customer who is not-engaged.

The not-engaged customer is a perfect switcher. He may be a customer in waiting for an emotional state to be created. Or he may be just insensitive to any emotional incentive and only value price. At the same time, he may not harbor any negative feelings, either; although many customers are clearly unimpressed with the experience of the brand, their connection to the brand is very limited and so is their engagement.

The not-engaged customer profile:

- Reveals a pattern of relative indifference to the current engagement capabilities of a brand or an organization.
- Inattentive and unresponsive to additional products or offers due to low purchase levels and usage of brands and products, or because of poor or nonexistent levels of per-

sonal interaction with the organization's service infra-structure.

The Actively Disengaged

This company is out to get as much as they can from cus-tomers; they mark up merchandise and then run "sales" to try to convince people that they're getting bargains. I take pleasure out of pointing out to them that lower prices are available elsewhere, just to show them how wise I am to their tricks. And I never think twice about complaining if the service or product isn't up to par, which they usually aren't. You want to know why? I hate these guys. I won't let my friends ever shop there.

Demonstrating active emotional disengagement and an-tagonism, these customers are the single most important marketing threat to an organization in terms of lost revenue and much higher servicing costs. If your organization is in-capable of restoring an emotional state, you are better off without them. Giving only a fraction of their purchase deci-sions to an organization, they may remain for either a short or a long period of time—but they will resist your efforts to gain their loyalty.

Rather than use, and benefit from, an organization's cus-tomer service department, actively disengaged customers are more likely to complain, disturb, and even sabotage it. No mat-ter how flexible your service infrastructure may be, these cus-tomers always require special attention, apply for more refunds, use more time of your service personnel, and, at their worst, can actually trigger a talent drain. If you cannot restore a positive emotional state, these customers should be subject to periodic pruning.

The actively disengaged customer profile:

- Account for the largest per customer service costs.
- Resentful, they will take advantage of any opportunity at their disposal to cause you harm, either directly or indirectly.
- Resistant to any attempt by your employees to switch from a negative perspective into a positive, restorative mood.
- Combining the relatively high costs with usually lower levels of revenue makes them very unprofitable.
- It requires a significant effort or improvement in the experience to turn them around. Some, in fact, never become engaged.

Customer Engagement: The Gallup Numbers

These are the percentages obtained from a survey taken across the United States from six different product and service categories:

- Fully engaged customers: 21 percent.
- Engaged customers: 21 percent.
- Not-engaged customers: 30 percent.
- Actively disengaged customers: 28 percent.

This is a fascinating set of numbers: The percentages for engaged employees and fully engaged customers are just about even. A deeper look into Gallup's recent multi-industry survey reveals differences in the percentages of customers falling into the four engagement categories.

The automobile industry reveals these numbers: 24 percent of its customers are fully engaged, 20 percent are engaged, 30 percent are not-engaged, and 26 percent are actively disengaged. The interesting phenomenon, however, is the wide range of customer engagement among the leading brands and manufacturers—ranging more than 20 percent.

Comparing the difference between U.S. domestic and imported vehicles, some interesting patterns emerge. Imported brands enjoy a much larger proportion of fully engaged (32 percent) and engaged customers (28 percent). They also have fewer actively disengaged customers (16 percent).

As with any number of industries in apparent turmoil, mass retail is an industry bedeviled by customer disengagement. Six out of every ten customers are disengaged, while only 19 percent of customers are fully engaged. The rest (22 percent) are simply engaged.

Not every retailer accepts this dire situation. One retailer possesses a proportion of disengaged customers similar to the industry's average, but it has been able to increase the proportion of its fully engaged buyers to 24 percent.

In the consumer electronics industry, the numbers are similar to those found among its retail cousins. Once more six of every ten customers are disengaged, 19 percent are fully engaged, and 22 percent are engaged. But again, the range in performance is amazing. Comparing two megaseller merchandise chains, one has more than twice the proportion of engaged customers than its rival in the fully engaged customer category.

These examples showcase the presence of two interrelated phenomena. First, it is painfully evident that most industries are operating at a fraction of their engagement potential. But second, despite the wide range in performance, some organizations have been able to hold significantly larger proportions of fully engaged customers in their customer base, which boosts their financial outcomes.

The CE[11] offers these industries—for the first time—a reliable way to monitor the engagement of their customers.

Look Inside to Solve the Outside Problem

Just as in the case of employee engagement, the Gallup study revealed the existence of a very wide range in terms of customer engagement within a company. Business units differ considerably in the degree to which they relate to their customers. This holds true even if they may offer the same products, at similar prices, in equal work environments and operate under the same marketing campaigns. The stunner here is that the range of performance *within* companies is usually much larger than the range of performance *between* companies.

This discovery hammers home the fact that there is no such thing as a "world-class" organization in terms of its customer engagement. Quite the contrary: No single organization stands out in Gallup's database as being especially qualified to either achieve or sustain a higher degree of customer engagement.

A good example of the importance of the internal range of performance is a major U.S. bank, which ranks among the nation's five largest. It offers a comprehensive range of financial products and services for consumers and small businesses through a substantial network of branches and ATMs as well as twenty-four-hour telephone and online channels.

But only 11 percent of this bank's customers are fully engaged. Twenty-two percent are engaged, 39 percent are not-engaged, and 28 percent are actively disengaged. The range of engagement performance within the bank has long-range economic implications. For a start, fully engaged customers hold balances that are on average $8,136 higher than those who are not-engaged or actively disengaged. Typically, they represent current revenue levels 13 percent higher than the other two lowest-engaged customer segments. The impact of this range to the bank's aggregate performance is staggering. An additional 1 percent of fully engaged customers would represent an increment of $155 million in balances alone.

This internal range of function deeply affects the bank's level of competitiveness within its industry as well. A comparison of the proportion of fully engaged customers (11 percent) with the industry's average (23 percent) means that the cost of underperforming in the vital area of customer engagement is costing this bank close to $2 billion annually in balances.

If this bank paid more attention to the engagement needs of its patrons, it could improve its finances even more. Currently, it costs this bank approximately $18 to correct a teller's accounting error. A 10 percent reduction in teller errors nets only approximately $220,000 in reduced costs. Yet a 10 percent reduction in the number of poorly performed employee–customer relations could save this bank over $200 million lost annually in personal balances alone.

Banks aren't the only organizations that require internal adjustments. Take a look at a leading global hospitality chain, which manages multiple hotel brands across many geographic regions. The Gallup study focused on the guest engagement program for one of its regional hotel chains, which includes approximately 150,000 members who pay an annual fee for a variety of lodging and restaurant benefits.

It turned out that only 8 percent of the members were fully engaged, 13 percent were engaged, 30 percent were not-engaged, and a large proportion—49 percent—were actively disengaged.

Once again, there was a clear benefit to engaging customers—and a real cost to disengaging them. For example, fully engaged members allocated a full 67 percent of their total annual lodging spending to this hotel chain, compared to 55 percent of engaged customers. But the percent of lodging spending allocated by not-engaged and actively disengaged customers combined was only 35 percent.

The financial implications of the actively disengaged members were very troubling. At an average cost per night of $150, for a typical annual stay of just over eighteen nights, actively disengaged members spent a paltry $950 compared with the sum spent by the others—$1,632.

Multiply the $682 difference by the number of members, and the sum reaches a very substantial amount. If this hospitality organization were able to reduce the level of customer disengagement by just 8 percent, this alone would represent an additional $8.67 million in lodging revenue each year.

Next, consider the example of an affinity/rewards credit card of one of the top five U.S. airlines. Using this card, members earn one mile in the airline's frequent flier program for every dollar they spend.

Again, the problem for this organization is the comparatively low level of customer engagement. Only 6 percent of its members are fully engaged and a quarter (25 percent) are engaged, but the majority of members are either not-engaged (45 percent) or actively disengaged (24 percent).

In dollars and cents, fully engaged members spend more than $3,600 per year using this card than disengaged members do. Fully engaged members also conduct a considerably larger number of transactions per year and hold balances that are almost 50 percent higher than the not engaged or disengaged members. With each fully engaged customer charging $2,834 more than all the other members annually, each additional 1 percent of fully engaged customers would add $142 million in total annual retail purchases and at least $1.5 in retail transactions.

Follow the Customer Engagement Path

To date, the largest proportion of fully engaged customers for any company worldwide is still less than 50 percent. This means that all organizations across the globe are running at a fraction of their potential, with severe economic implications to their financial outcomes.

In a time when CEOs and Wall Street economists are asking why soft numbers—which reflect people's attitudes, opinions, and preferences both as employees and customers—are becoming increasingly serious subjects of study, great organizations have learned that these numbers matter.

In today's business environment the ability to engage customers is the exception rather than the rule. The challenge for most organizations is how to make this process the norm rather than the rare exception. The list of requirements to make it happen includes the commitment of both corporate leadership and the front-line employee. Here's what the *great* organizations do:

Corporate commitment:

- Adopting one consistent metric and language—one that can yield valid comparisons among business units, brands, products, and time.
- Identifying the drivers of emotional attachment.
- Focusing on the experience and the engagement of the customer and holding every executive, manager, and employee accountable for how they impact the customer emotionally.
- Discovering the best practices and initiatives within the organization that stimulate emotional engagement.
- Continuously aligning the structure and the practices of the organization to best serve the engagement requirements of the customers.
- Guiding the organization's strategic response, as well as the tactical activities, of front-line managers and associates into coordinated action to enhance customer engagement.
- Empower and support all front-line employees and teams to continuously improve the customer's experience and level of engagement.

Commitment of front-line employees:

- Educating every employee on what truly engages customers emotionally.
- Increasing impact wherever and whenever customers are touched.
- Continuously identifying unique, personalized, and better ways to turn employee talent into richer customer experiences.

THE DISENGAGEMENT WARNING SIGNS YOU MUST HEED

The numbers don't lie here either. You must identify fully engaged, engaged, not-engaged, and actively disengaged customers, because they make a huge impact on your business every day. Unless the majority of your customers become either fully engaged or engaged—and stay that way—your business won't grow in a sustainable way.

If you want to compete successfully, you must engage your customers. This is the second lesson of emotional economics. If you are managing within a typical business environment, the reality is that the majority of your customers are not engaged. Probably more than a few of them are impacting negatively on your engaged employees to such an extent that those customers are actually hurting your business. When that happens, you must decide on the proper action to take, even if it seems drastic. Remember:

- The majority of your customers are not-engaged. More than half of the customers in the United States don't return to businesses, industries, or organizations on a regular basis because they don't feel an emotional connection to them.

- Not-engaged and actively disengaged customers cost money in time, service, and returns and in lost income potential.
- Fully engaged and simply engaged customers are vitally important to any company, because they keep returning. However, if their emotional link is either weakened or broken, they will leave.

Our findings suggest that the emotion-driven economy is several times bigger than the rational economy. So the obvious question for every organization is this: *What percentage of your organization is being to used to retain your customers emotionally?*

Remember: Disengagement is expensive. Engagement is profitable.

By understanding the economic implications of fully engaged, engaged, not-engaged, and actively disengaged customers, you have taken the tenth step on The Gallup Path.

CHAPTER 11

Managing the Emotional Economy

Three Is the Right Number

With years of documented study bolstered by the input of millions of employees, managers, and customers alike to refer to, we can safely say that maneuvering The Gallup Path successfully requires linking three elements in the proper sequence. The thirty-four talent streams flow into the Q^{12}, which is the direct route to the CE^{11}. Miss one connection and you miss them all. You can't get to where you want to go without following the specific directions. And you do want to arrive at the place where great organizations thrive. Why wouldn't you, when it's clear that:

- Talented individuals in the right role produce several times more than ordinary employees.
- Engaged work groups cost significantly less than their nonengaged counterparts and account for the lion's share of growth and profits.
- Their natural passion builds long-term customer relationships, securing the sustainability of their organization.
- Superior organizations have four times as many engaged employees as actively disengaged employees.

- Unleashing human potential yields a return on investment that ranges from 20 to 2,000 percent within an eighteen-month period. Evidence already exists of organizations investing $1 and seeing it grow into $250 within two years. The range in the return on investment varies depending on the type of industry, business scale, and, of course, leadership's commitment to this new economic and business model.

The study that we recently completed strongly speaks of a pattern employed by the world's most productive individuals, work groups, and organizations. While they vary in size, managerial style, industry, and location, these organizations meet the three requirements of superior performance time and time again.

1. Talent drives performance. Engage the talent of every employee.
Top performers share two important traits. First, they measure their performance in terms of objectively defined business outcomes and they use their talents as the key source for their individual strengths. Second, their superior performance is not explained by just how much they know factually, but by how they match up skills and knowledge with their natural talent as demanded continuously by their role. This implies a deep emotional connection with their individual hardwired talent.

The implications of this discovery are nothing short of revolutionary. Since superior performers always focus on attaining objectively defined results, the fixation on building colossal job architectures to describe, regulate, and legislate the work of employees is wrong. Talent—and only talent—should be a significant basis for hiring, selecting, and deploying employees, rather than just factual information or expertise. The work of talented employees reveals no relationship between job descriptions and finest performances.

Fine performances are the goal of every organization be-yond the obvious reasons of growth and profit. Today orga-nizations cannot and do not hold "power" over their employees. If you want to retain your best, acknowledge the best in them.

2. Engaged employees are your most productive people. Have managers engage all employees.
A recent international study sponsored by UBS, a Swiss bank, found that on average workers in the world's largest cities put in approximately 1,750 hours per year, with some regional and geographic variations. Multiply this figure by the number of employees working in an organization and what we get is an approximation of the total attention span assumed to impact productivity, revenues, and profits.

But that raises some very intriguing questions. How do these hours get spent? What specific events, mental processes, and activities are meant by "work"? And more important, what are the conditions that predict the superior performance of employees while "at work"?

The evidence gathered in the Gallup's database points to the twelve conditions—the Q^{12}—that characterize the most productive and energized workplaces. Contrary to con-ventional wisdom, the conditions that drive a productive workplace are not, as we have seen, a companywide issue but a locally based, business-unit-level issue and a reflec-tion of the local manager. These twelve conditions depend heavily on the organization's ability to establish meaningful employee–manager relationships.

These twelve conditions impact all business outcomes of the organization, including productivity, profitability, qual-ity, innovation, and safety. In addition to fueling the growth engine of the organization, these conditions are the most noteworthy human-related levers for cost reduction.

And engaged employees mean something else as well. They reflect a management style that doesn't try to "tell people what to do." Instead they understand that the very behaviors that employees exhibit are clues to their talents, a signal to follow to maximize those innate strengths. The economic value that great organizations create for their best employees is entirely emotional. It is built one employee at a time.

3. Engaged customers always come back for more. Engage customers so that all become profitable.
Real growth derives from both existing and new customers. But in the majority of the organizations we studied, the lion's share of their growth potential derives from existing customers. So our research focused on the conditions that drive repeat purchases and the larger sustainable sources of profit. We were surprised to find that what attracted these customers to their supplier was not the same as what engaged them. There was a major disconnect between purchase and repurchase.

What we did find was that engagement is an emotional bond formed by superior employee–customer interactions. Delivery supersedes promises every time.

These discoveries sharply contradict prevailing assumptions of most organizations' "theory of the consumer." According to these current perspectives, customer behavior (both initial purchase and repurchase) is the result of a careful rational examination of the benefits (incentives) presented by the available options. A customer is thought to simply select the option that "maximizes" value. The results of our study invalidate this theory altogether.

First of all, overwhelming evidence shows that customers always operate in conditions of incomplete information and uncertainty.

Second, the data show that customers don't always look for the best. Often they settle for options that offer a satisfactory solution to a problem or need.

Third, the evidence is consistent with recent discoveries in the field of neuroscience that indicate that feelings and emotions play a major role in people's repurchase decisions. It is not their rational but rather their emotional memory that counts.

Fourth, the evidence studied reveals that it isn't in making choices but in the framing of the alternatives for choices where the important moments for repurchase decisions occur. The evidence strongly indicates that low levels of customer engagement are consistent with low levels of emotional attachment. Connecting with deep-seated emotions of the customer is the best predictor of engagement.

It comes down to this: All customers must be treated as the individuals they are, and not as standardized blips on a statistical chart. There is only one factor that will impel customers to return to your brand or product or organization: the way they feel about you.

The era of establishing emotional connections solely or primarily with advertising or traditional marketing is gone—for good. That's why your organization needs to create effective emotional incentives one employee at a time. *This is your great challenge.*

Where Are You Going?

If you want to join the ranks of the great organizations, it's time to take an honest look at how you do business.

Where your *employees* are concerned:

1. How does your organization identify and evaluate the human potential of an individual employee?
2. How does it measure this potential?
3. What determines superior performance?
4. How is it linked to results?
5. How do your managers manage their work groups?

6. How does your organization identify the conditions that affect the contribution of a team?
7. How does it measure them?
8. What is the link between performance and business outcomes?

Where your *customers* are concerned:

1. How does your organization engage its customers?
2. How does your organization measure the emotional bond between customers and front-line employees?
3. How do you focus the talent of your employees to engage your customers and make them profitable?

REVIEW THE PATH

The ten steps of The Gallup Path are clearly laid out for you. Once you begin the journey into the emotion-driven economy, the sights along the way are going to change. You're going to view your employees in a whole new way—as talented people with unlimited potential. You're going to see your customers as complex emotional beings who long to forge links with what you can offer them. You can do this because you have seen:

1. The role emotions play in driving business outcomes.
2. That all your employees possess innate talents waiting to be engaged.
3. That engaging these unique talent combinations lead to profits and growth.
4. The power of Q^{12} and what it can do for your organization.
5. What managing to enhance and sustain employee engagement means.

6. The economic implications of the different types of employee engagement.
7. The power of CE[11] and how it can affect your brand, product, or organization.
8. The four states of customer engagement and how they will impact on your brand, product, or organization. It is the emotional memory that counts.
9. What managing to enhance and sustain customer engagement means.
10. The economic implications of the different types of customer engagement.

Now that you know the route to follow, you understand why you must follow The Gallup Path in its logical sequence.

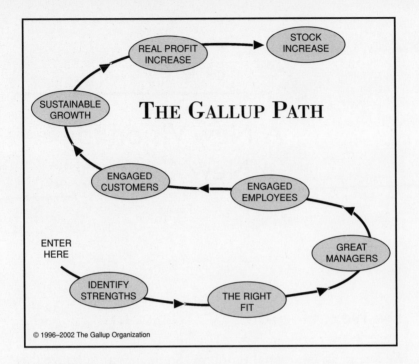

A New Vision for a New Century

The Next Horizon

We live in an emotional economy. Some may rationalize this fact; some may minimize it. But those who embrace it hold the future in their hands.

Great organizations of all types—profit, not-for-profit, public, private, employee and family owned—have taken notice of the new discriminating consumer they all serve. For the past twenty years the quality of both product and service delivery has improved four to five times over what it was previously. But through this improvement a challenge arose. The expectations of customers have risen to this new level as well. What used to exceed expectations now merely meets them.

Getting to the next improvement level that will drive competitive advantage is possible. To make it happen, it is imperative to tap into human nature through the ability of employees to engage every customer emotionally.

That's why it's time to set the human potential of your organization on the road to all it can be. Sticking to the old ways is about as productive as looking through the wrong end of a telescope and reducing everything to a microcosm.

Your organization contains priceless resources right now.

Widen your vision to see the people whom you pay who long to show you how talented they really are.

Cast your managers in the role of emotional "navigators" who will develop and appreciate engaged employees who, in turn, will connect with customers.

Expand your sights to the customers who want to stay and help you thrive, if only you show them how important they are to you.

It's time to see your world in a whole new way.

It's time to follow The Gallup Path.

To keep up with Gallup's latest discoveries in managing engaged employees and customers, please visit www.gallupjournal.com. This is the home page of the *Gallup Management Journal*.

THE GALLUP PATH CIRCUITRY
How many of these are turned 'ON' and how many 'OFF'

Graphic Design by: Julie Fienhold

34 Themes of Talent

Achiever
Activator
Adaptability
Analytical
Arranger
Belief
Command
Communication
Competition
Connectedness
Context
Deliberative
Developer
Discipline
Empathy
Consistency
Focus
Futuristic
Harmony
Ideation
Includer
Individualization
Input
Intellection
Learner
Maximizer
Positivity
Relator
Responsibility
Restorative
Self-assurance
Significance
Strategic
Woo

Q12

I know what is expected of me
I have the right materials and equipment
Opportunity to do what I do best
Recognition or praise for good work
Someone at work cares about me
Someone encourages my development
My opinions count
The mission/purpose of company/job is important
Coworkers committed to quality
I have a best friend at work
Someone has talked to me about my progress
Opportunities to learn and grow

CE11

Overall Satisfaction
Likelihood to repurchase
Likelihood to recommend
Name I can always trust
Always delivering on what they promise
Always treats me fairly
If a problem arises, satisfactory solution
I feel proud to be their customer
Always treats me with respect
Perfect company/product for people like me
I can't imagine a world without them

Business Outcomes

Sustainable Growth:
Significant increases in:
Sales volume
Customer retention
Same store sales overtime
Customer populations
Customer life cycles
Cross-business sales
New demand
Shorter purchasing cycles
Positive word-of-mouth

Real Profit Increase:
Cost reduction due to significant efficiencies in:
Per person performance
Communications
Delivery processes & systems
Employee claims
Employee turnover
Employee health
Number of effective workdays
Materials and equipment
Product quality
Productive employee cycles
Productivity
Production cycles
Selection of personnel
Service quality, processes & systems
Safety
Shrinkage
Telecommunications
Travel and transportation
Training costs
Utilities costs

Stock Increase (includes all of the above)

Endnotes

Introduction

1 For seven decades scientists at The Gallup Organization have studied the determinants of human behavior. As early as 1932 Dr. George Gallup began asking the hard question, "How do you know?" As a result of this long-term commitment, Gallup continually studies millions of customers every year. Just to give you an example: From 1997 to 2001, in the United States alone, The Gallup Organization interviewed 19,543,097 customers about practically every issue involving their opinions, attitudes, feelings, and behavior. Also, from 1991 to 2001 Gallup interviewed 1,610,303 professionals in every occupation, touching on every single aspect of their preferences, likes and dislikes, and, of course, lots about their workplace conditions. In terms of the individual assessment of talent and strengths, Gallup has conducted more than fifty thousand studies per year for more than two decades, totaling more than two million people studied individually. Gallup's knowledge has always grown by nourishing the current discoveries in the fields that relate to human nature, including the social sciences, psychology, economics, and neuroscience.

The results and insights presented in this book form a significant subgroup of the total number of individual studies conducted by Gallup spanning more than six decades.

2 Throughout this book the identities of individuals, organizations, and groups studied remain anonymous. Our emphasis in writing this book is on the dynamics that great organizations use to unleash their employees' human potential. Names and proprietary attributions of the people and organizations studied have been held confidential to protect their privacy.

Chapter One

1 Reichheld, Frederick F., and Leal Thomas (1996), *The Loyalty Effect: The Hidden Force Behind Growth, Profits and Lasting Value,* Cambridge, Massachusetts, Harvard Business School Press; Seligman, Martin (1994), *What You Can Change and What You Can't: Learning to Accept Who You Are,* New York, Knopf; Pinker, Steve (1997), *How the Mind Works,* New York, Norton; LeDoux, Joseph (2002), *Synaptic Self,* New York, Viking; Damasio, Antonio R. (1999), *The Feeling of What Happens: Body and Emotion in the Making of Consciousness,* New York, Harcourt; Manderfelt, Brett T., Gesuale, Brian, and Parizek, Gina (2001), *Human Capital,* Pipper Jaffray, US Bancorp, Equity Research, June.

2 For the past fifteen years our knowledge about the role of emotions in human learning and communication processes has expanded significantly, thanks to the discoveries made in the field of cognitive neuroscience. For more than a century, since the end of the nineteenth century when William James (1890) published his book *Principles in Psychology* (New York, Holt) suggesting that emotions were explained as mere bodily responses to external stimuli, the quest for describing emotion's role in human behavior remained an almost impossible task.

Emotions, we were told, were an elusive, subjective, and "hard to measure" part of human nature. For many leaders and scientists, emotions represented a "baggage of evolution," traits that humans shared with animals that interfered in the "more human" ability of rational thinking. Thanks to great technological advances in the measurement of brain functions and a resurgence in neurobiological research, emotions can today be described objectively as chemical reactions inside a human brain. There is also consensus among the scientific community in terms of the important role that emotions play in decision making; that they are a prerequisite for optimal mental states and rational thinking; and that a significant portion of our emotional learning is nonconscious.

Leading neuroscientist Antonio Damasio defines the basic framework of emotions as "a collection of neural dispositions in a set of brain regions located in the brainstem, hypothalamus, basal forebrain, amygdala, ventromedial prefrontal cortex and cingulated cortex." The process is fast and direct: A person receives a signal (for instance, seeing or hearing another person), and this signal travels from the sensory map (the senses) to the brain's emotional systems (such as the amygdala), which trigger a chemical reaction that in turn produces a feeling—either pleasant, such as happiness, surprise, pride, and excitement; or unpleasant, such as fear, sadness, anger, disgust, embarrassment, or guilt. *All this happens without any conscious or rational intervention.*

The accepted conclusions about emotions indicate that they are objective, measurable, and universal to all human beings. The implications of the effects of emotions as they relate to the workplace and to customer behavior are simple but powerful:

- Emotions set our highest-level goals, including how hard we work and how attached we stay to a brand or to an organization.
- Emotions take place outside our rational, willful aware-

ness; they cannot be imitated voluntarily; they constitute
our "emotional memory."
- Emotions drive our decision making, the emotional state
  of our conscious awareness.
- Emotional engagement increases the speed of learning.
- Emotional engagement increases memory retention.
- Emotional engagement allows the identification and the
  generation of emotions in others.

But emotions are the mechanisms of our mind least understood by management—hence the great opportunity for
organizations. Organizations have indirectly tried to trigger
emotions by using all types of symbols—brands, products,
technology. But the least applied and the most powerful
markers of emotions are human beings. Of all the sources of
emotional stimuli, the human voice and the human face are
the most effective emotional markers. Every human interaction elevates or downgrades the emotional state of a human
being. The bottom line is this: Employees and customers
have emotions, and these feelings drive their behavior. Organizations do not know this and have no clue how to generate emotional engagement—one human at a time. The
difference lies in being aware of these feelings and setting the
conditions to trigger the emotional mechanisms to generate
them and cultivate them among employees and customers.
And the best way to do so is through human interaction, the
fastest and most powerful trigger of emotional states. This is
the greatest challenge today.

The recent discoveries involve an important number of
contributions of neuroscientists around the world. The following list of contributions—most notably led by Antonio R.
Damasio (M. W. Van Allen Distinguished Professor and head
of the Department of Neurology at the University College of
Medicine in Iowa City) and Joseph LeDoux (Henry and Lucy
Moses Professor of Science at New York University's Center
for Neural Sciences)—is a partial list of the references that

we consider to be of significant value for readers interested in a more detailed review of the dynamic role of emotions, the nonconscious elements of emotional learning, the role of the amygdala and other brain systems in terms of processing and reactions to emotional stimuli, the neurotransmitters responsible for making us feel "good" or "bad" as a consequence of experimenting a particular emotional state, the primary and secondary sets of human emotions, and some implications for managers, employers, employees, and customers. As the work of these authors expands, the opportunity for organizations grows in creating increasing rational awareness of the nonconscious emotional components of human learning and communication.

Adolphs, R. Tranel, Hanna Damasio, and Antonio R. Damasio (1995), "Fear and the Human Amygdala," *Journal of Neuroscience* 15, pp. 5879–5892; Aggleton, John (ed.) (2000), *The Amygdala: A Functional Analysis*, New York, Oxford University Press; Damasio, R. Antonio (1995), *Descartes' Error: Emotion, Reason and the Human Brain*, London, Picador; Damasio, R. Antonio (1999), *The Feeling of What Happens*, NewYork, Free Press; Ekman, Paul, and Richard Davidson (eds.) (1994), *The Nature of Emotion*, New York, Oxford University Press; Lane, Richard, and Lynn Nadel (eds.) (2000), *Cognitive Neuroscience of Emotion*, New York, Oxford University Press; LeDoux, Joseph (1996), *The Emotional Brain*, New York, Simon & Schuster, (2002), *Synaptic Self*, New York, Viking; Rolls, Edmund (1999), *The Brain and Emotion*, New York, Oxford University Press; Scientific American (1999), *The Scientific American Book of the Brain*, NewYork, The Lyons Press; Gardner, Howard (1983), *Frames of Mind: The Theory of Multiple Intelligences*, New York, Basic Books; Gazzanica, Michael (ed.) (2000), *Cognitive Neuroscience: A Reader*, Malden, Massachusetts, Blackwell; Griffiths, P. E. (1997), *What Emotions Really Are*, Chicago, University of Chicago Press; Pinker, Steven (1997), *How the Mind Works*, New York, Norton; Rolls, Edmund T. (1999), *The Brain and*

Emotion, New York, Oxford University Press; Seligman, Martin (1998), *What You Can Change and What You Can't,* New York, Free Press.

The psychological interpretation of these findings is only beginning and can be found in the collective work of authors associated with the "Positive Psychology Movement." Rather than the traditional focus on pathology, weakness, and damage, their work begins to shed light onto the role of strengths and virtues, and to incorporate the study of positive work experiences, education, love, personal growth, and play. As Martin Seligman and Mihaly Csikszentmihalyi note in the introduction of the December 2000 issue of *American Psychologist,* researchers have discovered that "there are human strengths that act as buffers against mental illnesses: courage, future mindedness, optimism, interpersonal skill, faith, work ethic, hope, honesty, perseverance, and the capacity for flow and insight." As these researchers acknowledge, "much of the task of prevention in this century will be to create a science of human strength whose mission will be to understand and learn how to foster these virtues in young people." The recent discoveries in the fields of neurobiology, psychology, and economics have redefined our assumptions about human nature and mark the beginning of an important confluence of the human sciences once again in modern history. For an illustration of the role of positive emotions at the workplace, see the work of Barbara L. Frederickson (2000) "Why Positive Emotions Matter in Organizations" in *The Psychologist-Manager Journal* 4 (2), pp. 131–142.

Chapter Two

1 The call center case cited is one of dozens of studies conducted by Gallup in the past few years. The wide variations in terms of individual performance are constants in these studies, and they significantly affect business outcomes such

as number of successful calls made, number of attempts, increased productivity, decreased turnover, decreased training costs, increased spans of control, and customer retention and satisfaction. Superior performance is a function of having the right talent for the right job and working under the supervision of the right manager. For a more detailed account of various case studies, please review the contributions of Glenn Phelps, Gallup's call center practice manager, in the *Gallup Management Journal* 1, 2, and 3 (2001).

2 In 2001 The Gallup Organization helped 182,309 individuals discover their talents via StrengthsFinder, Gallup's Web-based talent profile and development tool. This number represents a total of 32,815,620 individual strength review items in 2001 alone. From 1999 to 2001 the total number of individuals who took StrengthsFinder is greater than 300,000. In addition, in 2001 alone Gallup conducted 38,736 in-depth developmental interviews. StrengthsFinder is now available in thirteen languages throughout the world. For a detailed review of the discovery process leading to the creation of StrengthsFinder, please consult Buckingham, Marcus, and Donald Clifton (2001), *Now, Discover Your Strengths,* New York, The Free Press.

3 For a succinct review of the limitations embedded in the "competency" model, please review Buckingham, Marcus (2002), "Don't Waste Time and Money," on the Web site of the *Gallup Management Journal* at http://www.gallupjournal.com/CA/ee/ 20011203.asp.

Chapter Three

1 The case studies showcasing talent's impact on business outcomes are offered with the intention to illustrate the di-

rect link between talent and superior performance. These studies are a minuscule proportion of the literally hundreds of studies that Gallup has conducted on this subject for a period spanning more than three decades and totaling more than two million professionals in every occupation.

2 The description of the meta-analytical procedures to estimate the contribution of talent to business outcomes appeared in Schmidt, Frank L., and Mark Rader (1999), "Exploring the Boundary Conditions for Interview Validity: Meta-Analytic Validity Findings for a New Interviewing Type," *Personnel Psychology* 52.

Chapter Four

1 Phil Esposito was interviewed by Gallup in Minneapolis on December 23, 1981. His enormous talent was studied as a result of this interview. Most references about Phil Esposito included in this chapter are taken from the verbatim of this interview with Mr. Esposito's explicit consent.

2 For detailed reference to the discovery process leading to the formulation of Q^{12}, please consult Buckingham, Marcus, and Curt Coffman (1999), *First, Break All the Rules,* New York, Simon & Schuster.

Chapter Five

1 A significant part of Gallup's mission is helping individuals, groups, and organizations grow their strengths. In practice, this takes various forms. One of them is individualized learning opportunities offered by the Gallup University. A particularly relevant example of these opportunities is the Great Manager Program, which has been designed specifi-

cally with the purpose of helping managers and organizations develop the understanding and the actions needed to establish the twelve conditions of an engaged workplace. In 2001 alone, more than twelve thousand professionals participated in courses offered by Gallup.

Chapter Six

1 The Gallup Organization conducts quarterly polls of employed Americans (eighteen years and older). The polls quantify and track the level of national employee engagement and other workplace issues (involving random samples of at least one thousand working Americans each quarter). Ongoing findings are reported in the *Gallup Management Journal* and through press releases. Sample sizes and dates for non-U.S. countries reported in this book: Canada n = 1,006 (August 2001); Chile n = 410 (April 2001); France n = 1,004 (2001); Germany n = 2,009 (August 2001); Great Britain n = 832 (May 2001); Singapore n = 1,022 (August 2001); Japan n = 606 (June 2001). Results with sample sizes of n = 1,000 have a margin of error of plus or minus 3 percent at a confidence level of 95 percent.

2 A discussion of the concept, statistical techniques, and results derived from meta-analysis constitutes appendix B of this book.

Chapter Seven

1 An important number of studies dating back to the early 1990s have quantified the disproportionately larger profits and source of growth represented by repeat customers. Examples of this type of analysis include Rogers, Dr. Martha (1993), *The One to One Future*, New York, Doubleday; Reichheld,

Fred, and Earl Sasser, "Zero Defections: Quality Comes to
Service," *Harvard Business Review,* September–October
1990; Raphel, Murray, "Bring Them Alive: How to Get Back
Those Customers Who Left for the Competition Jungle," *Di-
rect Marketing,* May 1990; Advisory Board Company
(1991), "Retail Customer Retention: Economic Analysis";
Clamsy, Kevin, and Robert Shulman (1990), *The Marketing
Revolution,* New York, Harper Business Books; Heskett,
James L., Leonard Schlesinger, and Earl Sasser (1997), *The
Service Profit Chain: How Leading Companies Link Profit
and Growth to Loyalty, Satisfaction, and Value,* New York,
The Free Press.

2 The "theory of the rational consumer" assumed individuals in the role of economic agents who have complete sets of
preferences and can gather complete and free information,
minimizing their degree of uncertainty. Customers are assumed to make rational choices according to their preferences so as to optimize their utility. Their behavior is
considered rational provided that they arrange the necessary
means to reach a given goal. The origin of the preferences,
however, is generally not examined. This theory is under severe scrutiny and criticism for its flawed assumptions about
the drivers of human behavior, as these are generally "taken
for granted" or "assumed to be universal." At the time when
it was proposed, this vision was heavily influenced by be-
haviorism, which generally viewed customers' conduct as
being a direct response to a same set of circumstances (everyone reacting just the same) and as being subject to predeter-
mined homogeneous situations of signal processing and
interpretation. But more important, this theory reduces
human nature almost exclusively to our ability to "think logically," assuming that humans use this logic as a determinant
of their behavior. The human mind was assumed to be a
"black box": too intricate an object of analysis. Within this
perspective, learning and image processing were assumed to

be homogeneous, so customers were assumed to hold the same view of the world. They were viewed as utility-seeking individuals, rationally looking for the best possible combination of value in their purchasing actions. Aiming and finding the necessary criteria to maximize value and minimize resources, the conflicting actions of individual customers were assumed to be balanced by the forces of perfect competition, which, according to the neoclassical paradigm, generated a state of general economic equilibrium. This theory fails to account for the fact that every human being is unique and different in terms of her mental filter and image-processing and communication capabilities. And last but not least, this theory fails to address the important effect of emotions on rational thought and customer behavior.

The "theory of the consumer" bears distinct assumptions derived from the neoclassical economic theory, whose foundations trace back to the work of Eugen E. Slutsky (1915), "On the Theory of the Budget of the Consumer," in American Economic Association, *Readings in Price Theory,* chapter 2, George Allen & Unwin (1952), pp. 27–56; Ricks, J. R., "A Reconsideration of the Theory of Value, Part I," *Economica* 1 (February 1, 1934), pp. 52–76; Allen, R. G. D., "A Reconsideration of the Theory of Value, Part II—A Mathematical Theory of Individual Demand Functions," *Economica* 2 (May 1934), pp. 196–219; Hotelling, Harold, "Demand Functions with Limited Budgets," *Econometrica* III (1) (January 1935), pp. 66–78.

The "revealed preferences" model can be traced back to the classicists, starting with the bright formulations of Samuelson, Paul A., "Consumption Theory in Terms of Revealed Preference," *Economica* XV (60) (November 1948), pp. 243–253; Houthakker, H. S., "Revealed Preference and the Utility Function," *Economica* XVII (66) (May 1950), pp. 159–174; McKenzie, Lionel, "Demand Theory without a Utility Index," *Review of Economic Studies* XXIV (3) (June 1957), pp. 185–189. To this day the models of "revealed preferences" constitute a widely practiced form of customer choice analysis. The problem, of course, is that in the majority of cases the users do not pay sufficient attention to their assumptions, with the consequence of measuring very detailed responses to a product offering but lacking the adequate understanding of what drives customer behavior.

Within economics, the critique of the "rational consumer" and the "revealed preferences" paradigm is as diverse as it is prolific. The serious problems relate to the grossly flawed assumptions underpinning it: (a) Customers are not utility-maximizing economic agents; (b) they do not only follow their reason but are also influenced by their emotions; (c) the important moment is not only their "choice" but the moments of framing the alternatives to making a choice; (d) customers operate in conditions of limited knowledge and uncertainty; (e) perhaps more important, individuals are uniquely different in terms of how they perceive the world around them, process and interpret mental images, and particularly think, relate, strive, and impact others around them. The innate predispositions that human beings have to do what each does best, to seek the advice of others whom each trusts, to comply with the expectations of a significant relationship, to be part of a group, and to be emotionally attached are issues largely ignored by the neoclassical "theory of the consumer."

The classic criticism can be traced back to the Austrian School, which in the 1930s started debating the crucial role played by diversified knowledge in decision-making processes, particularly represented by Menger, Karl (1967), "The Role of Uncertainty in Economics," in *Essays in Mathematical Economics in Honor of Oskar Morgenstern,* edited by M. Shubik, Princeton, New Jersey, Princeton University Press, and *Principles in Economics* (1976), Institute for Humane Studies; Hayek, F. A., "Economics and Knowledge," *Economica* IV (13), pp. 96–105, and "The Use of Knowledge in Society," *American Economic Review* 35 (4) (1945), pp. 519–530. These two authors demanded the study of the nonconscious nature of human decisions. This critique was further extended by the work of Herbert A. Simon (*Models of Man*, 1957, New York, Wiley; and *Models of Bounded Rationality: Empirically Grounded Economic Reason*, 1997, MIT Press), who argued that individuals do not necessarily aim to "maximize" but rather to "satisfy" their expectations of value and utility. In practical terms, he meant that individuals use information and knowledge to solve practical problems instead of aiming to gain full and complete expertise in making "rational" decisions. A thorough review of the critiques of the "rational" theory of the consumer can be found in Rizzello, Salvatore (1999), *The Economics of the Mind*, Edward Elgar Publishing. The critical problem for most criticisms of the neoclassical economic theory of the consumer is that they are only beginning to incorporate into their conceptual framework the recent discoveries about the intricate interplay between reason and emotion in human behavior—how the human mind works.

Chapter Eight

1 Emotional engagement of customers requires that organizations define the creation, cultivation, or restoration of emotional states as the "right" outcome, rather than limit their focus to the question of whether or not the functional aspects of the customer interaction were performed according to plan. The CE[11] metric has been designed to diagnose the basic four emotional states in each customer.

Chapter Nine

1 The study of the actions that great managers undertake to positively impact employees' abilities to create, sustain, and

restore emotional states constitutes an important component of Gallup's curriculum, particularly within the Great Manager Program. Particular emphasis is given to the issue of identifying and measuring the emotional states of customers, since feelings are not usually easily observable. A significant effort must be made by managers and employees alike not only in the definition of the right actions but also in devising the diagnostics to identify signals in the everyday life of the organization through objective and reliable methods.

Chapter Ten

1 The case studies presented in this chapter form a very small group of the much larger number of studies conducted in the area of customer engagement. Additional reviews are presented regularly in the *Gallup Management Journal*.

Managerial Talent, Employee Engagement, and Business Unit Performance

This appendix reviews and explores relationships among managerial talent, employee engagement, and business unit–level performance. Findings from several data sets highlight two critical areas in the context of many external factors that, it is argued, can substantially improve the probability of business unit–level success. These are: a) selecting managers with the talent to efficiently manage people and processes, and b) building an environment that supports employee engagement. Together these factors explain complementary and unique variance in business unit–level performance within organizations.

This appendix reviews two previously reported meta-analytic bodies of evidence. One is developed around an understanding of managerial talents (recurring patterns of

A more detailed description of the content of this appendix appeared in Harter, J. K. (2000) "Manager Talent, Employee Engagement, and Business Unit Performance" in *The Psychologist-Manager Journal* 4 (2) pp. 215–224. This summary is printed with permission of the publisher, Society of Psychologists in Management. Copyright 2000.

thought, feeling, and behavior that include combinations of various personality and General Mental Ability constructs) and another developed around an understanding of workplace employee engagement (a substantial predictor of business outcomes and satisfaction) to understand their joint effects on business unit performance. A third meta-analysis studying the relationship between managerial talent (described later) and employee engagement will be introduced.

Genetic and Situational Influences on Work Behavior

There are several bodies of contemporary evidence from multiple disciplines that give us clues about how to efficiently lead and manage the workplace to achieve high levels of performance. Clearly, proper selection in matching people with jobs is critical.

Schmidt and Hunter (1998), for example, reviewed eighty-five years of research findings on employee selection methods in personnel psychology. Among the top predictors of later job performance were general mental ability tests and structured interviews. Constructs imbedded within these measures include analytical reasoning, problem-solving, and certain personality and integrity constructs (structured interviews likely provide additive prediction beyond mental ability in the form of the personality and integrity constructs they measure).

The fact that these constructs predict later job performance provides a possible explanation for their enduring nature. Genetic research on individual differences highlights the importance of understanding and positioning people, as opposed to trying to change their inherent nature. In fact, studies of identical twins reared apart show high heritability of personality and intelligence, once corrected for measurement error. A high percentage of variation in intelligence and personality characteristics has been found to be associated with genetic variation (Bouchard, Lykken, McGue, Segal, and Tellegen, 1990; Bouchard, 1997). While these findings certainly do not indicate that people do not grow and progress, they hint at something about efficiency in managing people: How people grow and progress is at least dynamically interwoven with who they are to begin with. The effect of genetic makeup on job satisfaction appears positive, but less strong (Arvey, Bouchard, Segal, and Abraham, 1989). Therefore, it appears there is more room for managerial influence in the job satisfaction realm and perhaps other related affective constructs. Understanding how each individual's talents (the possibly inherent or recurring patterns of thought, feeling, and behavior) can most efficiently be channeled to achieve success appears to be a critical factor. Managers are in the best position to contribute to this.

Managers appear to affect their business unit's performance both through their inherent style of management and through the employees themselves. Understanding the talents that differentiate successful from less successful managers represents one important body of evidence. Another is how the level at which employees are engaged relates to business unit success. But to what extent does managerial talent alone explain employee engagement, and what are the shared and unique effects of each on the performance of the business unit? This article will explore the influences of each of these variables in relations to business unit performance by reviewing meta-analytic evidence and combining this evidence into a multiple regression analysis.

Managerial Talent Versus Leadership Influences

First, I will briefly discuss The Gallup Organization's research on the relationship between employee engagement and business outcomes. Second, I will provide a brief review of the business unit–level performance relatedness of transformational leadership and Gallup managerial research under the heading of "managerial talent." Third, multicompany evidence is presented, addressing the relationship between Gallup's structured interview measures of managerial talent and employee engagement. Combining these bodies of evidence, we gain a clearer understanding of managerial talent and employee engagement individually, and in relation to business unit performance.

Gallup Workplace Management Evidence on Employee Engagement

The Gallup Q^{12} Impact Management program (Harter and Schmidt 2000, Buckingham and Coffman, 1999) makes use of an instrument designed to measure the quality of people-related management for work groups and business units—the Gallup Q^{12}. As an instrument, it has evolved from over twenty-five years of management research and the study of success across a wide variety of workplace types. Included in Q^{12} measurement instrumentation are an overall satisfaction item and twelve items measuring the manageable facets related to employee engagement (antecedents to satisfaction and other outcomes) (Harter, 2000; Fleming, 2000; Buckingham and Coffman, 1999). Instead of simply asking employees how satisfied they are with various aspects of their jobs (with their pay, benefits, supervisor, co-workers, responsibilities, for instance), the Q^{12} instead asks employees to rate the extent to which their basic workplace needs are met. Kahn's (1990) conceptualization of cognitive and emotional engagement provides a close approximation of what is measured with the Q^{12}. Employees are emotionally connected to their work group and organization and cognitively vigilant when their basic needs are met.

Furthermore, Fredrickson's (1998, 2000) broaden-and-build model of positive emotion provides yet another theoretical understanding of the roots of engagement and how positive emotions can broaden the thought and action repertoires of individuals, which helps them build enduring resources (relationships, materials, friendships, creative solutions, and ideas). I argue that when employees' basic needs are met and positive emotions are experienced more frequently, this "broadening and building" becomes one source of differentiation between highly productive and less productive work groups. Criteria used in selecting items encompassing the Q^{12} include comprehensiveness of item coverage, performance-relatedness of items, and actionability (that is, behaviors under the control of the manager and employee). The items included in the Q^{12} are provided in Table 1.

The design and performance-relatedness to business unit–level outcomes of the Q^{12} are detailed in a recent Gallup technical report (Harter and Schmidt, 2000). Business units within companies in these combined samples scoring above the median on the Q^{12} had a 70 percent higher likelihood of success (composite of customer loyalty, employee turnover, and financials) in comparison to business units below the median. Business units above the median on employee engagement average one-half standard deviation higher performance in comparison to business units below the median on employee engagement.

Range within Companies

Over the past three years, Gallup's Q^{12} database has grown to include over three hundred thousand work groups and business units. One interesting finding from this database is the range in employee engagement that exists within nearly every company across work groups. In fact, in the average company, the standard deviation of employee engagement is 75 percent of the standard deviation across all work groups in all companies in the database. In census surveys of companies (which average 77 percent response rates), sampling error is quite low or nearly nonexistent. As such, the range that exists within most companies represents largely real group-level differences in how employees perceive their workplaces. Given the performance-relatedness of employee engagement, this finding highlights an important opportunity to understand how success occurs at the work-group level in nearly any organization, and how to replicate it.

Managerial Talent

Possible solutions to the wide differences in employee engagement within most organizations include identifying characteristics of effective managers and selecting for or developing these characteristics. The body of literature on transformational leadership offers insight into the characteristics of effective leaders and managers (Bass, 1985, 1990, 1995, 1997, 1998). As opposed to a more transactional approach to leadership, an approach in which leaders prescribe for employees what to do, transformational leadership involves leaders broadening and elevating the interests of their employees. This can be accomplished by creating awareness and acceptance of the purposes and mission of the organization and looking beyond self-interest to the interest of the group as a whole. Transformational leadership measures include estimates of constructs such as charisma, intellectual stimulation, and individualized consideration. A study by Lowe, Kroeck, and Sivasubramaniam (1996) indicates correlations—ranging from 0.26 for intellectual stimulation to 0.25 for charisma—to "hard" measures of organizational performance.

A separate body of evidence accumulated by The Gallup Organization, including studies of thousands of managers and leaders (involving both concurrent and predictive validity studies) suggests some convergent and unique qualities of highly effective management (Schmidt and Rader, 1999; Buckingham and Coffman, 1999).

The role of a manger of people, while diverse in terms of specific positions and companies, consists of a few fundamental aspects. Highly effective managers focus on outcomes by offering clear direction to employees. They provide measurable outcomes to stimulate, and help employees to nonsubjectively understand, the fulfillment of objectives. They are flexible—they focus on the uniqueness of each individual they manage while maintaining objectivity around the ultimate outcomes. They manage through people to obtain the desired outcomes. They activate others to contribute to a common cause or purpose and they initiate processes that lead the group to greater efficiency while obtaining the desired outcomes. They confront obstacles to advance the purpose of the group they lead. They are great arrangers of people and resources.

The predictive validity of a structured interview technique used to measure a composite of these managerial talents (identified through job analysis) was analyzed by Schmidt and Rader (1999). Meta-analytic predictive validities across criterion types and job types in this study were 0.40. A subset of managers was included in this meta-analysis (which was based on three studies) with a predictive validity (based on supervisory ratings of business unit performance) of 0.27. Schmidt and Rader (1999) concluded that, due to factors inherent in meta-analysis (number of studies, alternative specific methodologies, etc.), that this estimate may be lower than the true value. Other reasons to suspect that this set of studies may underestimate relationships include reliance on supervisor evaluations, which are but one perspective on a manager's performance, and may exclude consideration of such directly measurable factors as employee turnover, customer satisfaction, and financials. Therefore, it is reasonable to assume that the 0.27 predictive validity estimate is a conservative, lower bound estimate of the true relationship between this measure of talent and overall managerial performance.

Taking into account the transformational leadership meta-analysis (Lowe et al., 1996) and the Schmidt and Rader (1999) meta-analysis, it appears the true relationship between identified measures of managerial talent and overall business performance is likely to be in the 0.30 range, conservatively, and likely higher. Considering the number of factors that can influence business unit–level performance, including economic uncontrollables, competitive proximity, seasonality, and other factors, this presumed relationship appears to be a substantial one. The size of effect suggested by this relationship represents approximately one-half standard deviation difference in performance between business units above the median on managerial talent compared to those below the median.

The Relationship between Managerial Talent and Employee Engagement

To understand the complementary and unique contribution of managerial talent and employee engagement in explaining business unit–level performance, it is necessary to understand the relationship between managerial talent and employee engagement. Extremely effective managers certainly appear to have a combination of various mental abilities and personality characteristics that relate to success (Schmidt and Hunter, 1998; Schmidt and Rader, 1999; Bass, 1985, 1990, 1995, 1997, 1998; Buckingham and Coffman, 1999). Many of the qualities of great management are convergent with the definition of "employee engagement" described earlier (clear expectations, materials and equipment, caring about and rewarding individuals, developing a common purpose, etc.) as well.

Five studies of the relationship between composite managerial talent (as described earlier) and employee engagement were identified and included in a cross-company Gallup analysis. The process for conducting and scoring the structured interview used in this research is described in Schmidt and Rader (1999). Each of the five studies included in these analyses included direct report ratings of the quality of their work environment, measures convergent with the Q^{12} composite measure. This article will not provide a full description of the research methodologies. Rather, readers are encouraged to refer to the following sources for both background information and detailed descriptions of more recent meta-analytic methods: Schmidt (1992); Hunter and Schmidt (1990); Lipsey and Wilson (1993); Bangert-Drowns (1986); and Schmidt, Hunter, Pearlman, and Rothstein-Hirsh (1985).

The five studies comprise the current cross-sample combined analyses, which collectively include 421 managers and covered a range of industries, including retail, restaurants, healthcare, and manufacturing (Table 2), each collected by The Gallup Organization from different companies. These datasets were collected as Gallup client data. Each study included all managers available, representing a broad range on measures of managerial talent and employee engagement for each company. Meta-analysis and validity generalization techniques are designed to understand true relationships and their variability across studies, or in this case, across diverse organizations in which the same data-collection methods were used. Results (shown in the lower portion of Table 2) indicate that the mean observed correlation of managerial talent with employee engagement was 0.31 (Pearson r prior to correction for attenuation) with a standard deviation of 0.09. After correcting for sampling error, the standard deviation was 0.00, indicating generalizability (or consistent correlations) across the five organizations studied. The true validity (correcting for measurement error in the employee engagement measure using text/retest reliability) reported in Harter, Schmidt (2000) was 0.35. The true score correlation (correcting for measurement error in both the independent and dependent variable) was 0.39. Table 3 summarizes the correlations reviewed and studied in this article: First, the relationship between managerial talent and employee engagement; second, the relationship between managerial talent and business unit–level performance (an estimate from meta-analyses provided by Lowe et al., 1996; and Schmidt and Rader, 1999); and third, the relationship between employee engagement and composite business unit–level performance found in the cross-sample Gallup data. These estimates provide corrections for dependent variable measurement error. Among the three relationships studied, the relationship was strongest for managerial talent with employee engagement (rxy = 0.35), followed by managerial talent with performance (rxy = 0.30), and employee engagement with performance (rxy = 0.26). Entering the coefficients from the upper portion of Table 3 into a regression equation, it is possible to consider the unique contributions of managerial talent and employee engagement to business-unit performance.

The lower portion of Table 3 provides the multiple regression beta weights and multiple correlation. Combining a measure of managerial talent and employee engagement resulted in a multiple R of 0.35 (SE = 0.05). This implies that managerial talent is related to employee engagement, but also that each of the two measures provides an independent contribution to the prediction of business unit performance (both with positive beta values). One possible reason for this is that, although managers can take the lead in setting the stage for an engaged workplace, other employees and other factors are likely to influence employee engagement and how it contributes to overall business unit performance. These results suggest that managers may influence performance directly through the application of their inherent talents and indirectly through those who report to them.

Discussion

One implication for the psychologist-manager is that the efficient management of people should include an understanding of the talents of persons selected for management positions. Furthermore, providing a supportive environment that complements managers' individuality in a way that helps them grow in areas of strength is important for both the manager and the employee. Measuring employee engagement as an outcome for managers and educating managers on how to improve the engagement level of their associates is critical. The joint relationship of managerial talent and employee engagement provides a stronger indication of business unit–level performance than either one does alone. When organizations select talented managers, the engagement of their employees in the business objectives is more likely.

Further research should focus on more specific clarification of the characteristics (personality, values, mental ability, etc.), in addition to charisma and individualized consideration, that lead to business unit–level performance. Some management characteristics probably relate to employee engagement at a higher level than others. Also, some characteristics or practices of managers are probably related to particular aspects of engagement at higher levels than others (that is, expectations, feeling cared about, discussion or progress made). For instance, managers with operational talents may have greater clarity of expectations, and may be better suited to provide materials and equipment, and to discuss progress with employees on a regular basis. Managers with relationship-building talents may do a better job of building a sense of caring and teamwork. These are all patterns that should be explored further in individual studies and meta-analytic, cross-organizational research. The implications of such research relate to how managers with varying talents develop and partner with others to meet the needs of their employees and of the business itself.

The findings reported in this study are admittedly broad in their potential for interpretation. For instance, the measures of "managerial talent," "employee engagement," and "performance" were composites of multiple facets and performance criteria. Therefore, the need for a more specific understanding of the relationships among the multiple facets within these broad constructs rests on further development of databases across companies.

Further work should also focus on which elements of the various definitions of talent are changeable and which are not. Research on transformational leadership indicates that, from employees' perspectives, its components are at least somewhat changeable. How long and under what conditions and investments they remain changeable are salient follow-up questions, however. Components of managerial talent that are convergent with mental ability and personality may be less changeable. In such circumstances, an efficient practice would center on how individual talents could be understood and applied to create positive experiences for the individual, the people being managed, and the business itself.

Conclusion

I will close with one final note regarding the current labor market and the ability to select and develop managers: Currently, it is difficult to be selective for many employee positions (due to current economic circumstances of low unemployment rates and increasing turnover rates). One exception to this rule may be the selection and development of managers. Since employees outnumber managers in most companies (often by ten to one or more) there may be ample opportunity to carefully position the right nonmanagers into people-management positions. One future challenge of the psychologist-manager may relate to learning the talents of employees and positioning them so that they can maximize who they are, in some cases growing into managerial positions. Additionally, it appears to be critical to provide a supportive environment that complements employees' individuality in a way that helps them grow in areas of strength. Realistically, all large organizations will have a range of both managerial talent and employee engagement across the work groups they manage. It is important to treat each of these as ongoing initiatives, with efficient measurement, to understand growth and progress. Business growth is one potential and realistic consequence.

—James K. Harter, Ph.D.
The Gallup Organization

TABLE 1
Items Comprising the Gallup Q^{12}

1. I know what is expected of me at work
2. I have the materials and equipment I need to do my work right
3. At work, I have the opportunity to do what I do best every day
4. In the last seven days, I have received recognition or praise for doing good work
5. My supervisor, or someone at work, seems to care about me as a person
6. There is someone at work who encourages my development
7. At work my opinions seem to count
8. The mission or purpose of my company makes me feel my job is important
9. My associates or fellow employees are committed to doing quality work
10. I have a best friend at work
11. In the last six months, someone at work has talked to me about my progress
12. This last year, I have had opportunities to learn and grow at work

TABLE 2
Summary of Studies Included in Cross-Company Analyses

Study	n
(1) Retail Managers	101
(2) Restaurant Managers	29
(3) Restaurant Managers	41
(4) Healthcare Managers	50
(5) Manufacturing Managers	200
Total	421

Meta-analysis Statistics

Observed r = 0.31	Observed SD = 0.09	True Validity = 0.35
True Validity SD = 0.00	Rho = 0.39	Rho SD = 0.00

TABLE 3
Summary of Cross-Company Correlations and Multiple Regression Statistics

Meta-Analytic Correlations Relationship	r	Reference
Managerial Talent to Employee Engagement	0.35	Current Study
Managerial Talent to Business Unit Performance	0.30	Schmidt & Rader (1996)
Employee Engagement to Business Unit Performance	0.26	Harter & Schmidt (2000)

Multiple Regression Statistics Independent Variable	Beta	SE[a]
Managerial Talent	0.25	0.06
Employee Engagement	0.18	0.06
Multiple r	0.35	0.05

assuming 421 managers (the lowest sample size in the meta-analysis)

References

Arvey, R. D., Bouchard, T. J., Jr., Segal, N. L. & Abraham, L. M. (1989). Job satisfaction: environmental and genetic components. *Journal of Applied Psychology,* 74, 187–192.

Bangert-Drowns, R. L. (1986). Review of developments in meta-analytic method. *Psychological Bulletin,* 99, 3, 388–399.

Bass, B. M. (1985). *Leadership and Performance beyond Expectations.* New York: Free Press.

Bass, B. M. (1995). Theory of transformational leadership redux. *Leadership Quarterly,* 6, 463–478.

Bass, B. M. (1997). Does the transactional-transformational leadership paradigm transcend organizational and national boundaries? *American Psychologist,* 52, 130–139.

Bass, B. M. (1998). *Transformational Leadership*. Mahwah, NJ: Lawrence Erlbaum Associates.

Bass, B. M. & Stodgill, R. M. (1990). *Bass & Stodgill's Handbook of Leadership: Theory, Research and Managerial Applications*. (3rd ed.) New York: Free Press.

Bouchard, T. J., Jr. (1997). Genetic influence on mental abilities, personality, vocational interests, and work attitudes. *International Review of Industrial and Organizational Psychology*, 12, 373–395.

Bouchard, T. J., Lykken, D. T., McGue, M., Segal, N. L., & Tellegen, A. (1990). Sources of human psychological differences: The Minnesota study of twins reared apart. *Science*, 250, 223–228.

Buckingham, M. & Coffman, C. (1999). *First, Break All the Rules: What the World's Greatest Managers Do Differently*. New York: Simon & Schuster.

Fleming, J. H. (2000). Relating employee engagement and customer loyalty to business outcomes in the retail industry. *The Gallup Research Journal*, 2000, 103–115.

Fredrickson, B. L. (1998). What good are positive emotions? *Review of General Psychology*, 2, 300–319.

Fredrickson, B. L. (2000). Why positive emotions matter in organizations: Lessons from the broaden-and-build model. *Psychologist-Manager Journal*, 4, 131–142.

Harter, J. K. (2000). The linkage of employee perceptions to outcomes in a retail environment—cause and effect? *The Gallup Research Journal*, Winter/Spring 2000, 25–38.

Harter, J. K. & Schmidt, F. L. (2000). Validation of a performance-related and actionable management tool: A meta-analysis and utility analysis. *Gallup Technical Report*. Lincoln, NE: The Gallup Organization.

Hunter, J. E. & Schmidt, F. L. (1990). *Methods of Meta-Analysis: Correcting Error and Bias in Research Findings.* Newbury Park, CA: Sage.

Kahn, W. A. (1990). Psychological conditions of personal engagement and disengagement at work. *Academy of Management Journal,* 33, 692–724.

Lipsey, M. W. & Wilson, D. B. (1993). The efficacy of psychological, educational and behavioral treatment. *American Psychologist,* 48, 1181–1209.

Lowe, K. B., Kroeck, K. G., & Sivasubramaniam, N. (1996). Effectiveness correlates of transformation and transactional leadership. A meta-analytic review of the MLQ literature. *Leadership Quarterly,* 7, 385–425.

Schmidt, F. L. (1992). What do data really mean? Research findings, meta-analysis and cumulative knowledge in psychology. *American Psychologist,* 47, 1173–1181.

Schmidt, F. L. & Hunter, J. E. (1998). The validity and utility of selection methods in personnel psychology: Practical and theoretical implications of 85 years of research findings. *Psychological Bulletin,* 124, 262–274.

Schmidt, F. L., Hunter, J. E., Pearlman, K., Rothstein-Hirsch, H. (1985). Forty questions about validity generalization and meta-analysis. *Personnel Psychology,* 38, 697–798.

Schmidt, F. L. & Rader, M. (1999). Exploring the boundary conditions for interview validity: Meta-analytic validity findings for a new interview type. *Personnel Psychology,* 52, 445–464.

APPENDIX B

Employee Engagement, Satisfaction, and Business Unit–Level Outcomes: A Meta-Analysis

This report is a summary of a larger technical report produced by The Gallup Organization.

This paper summarizes the results of an updated meta-analysis of the relationship between employee workplace perceptions and business unit outcomes, based on currently available data collected with Gallup clients. The focus of this study is on the twelve statements included in Q^{12}. These twelve items—which were selected because of their importance at the business unit or work-group level—measure employee perceptions of the quality of people-related management practices in their business units. This report provides an update of previous research reported by Harter and Schmidt (2000) and Harter, Schmidt, and Hayes (2002).

Background Behind Q^{12}

The history of the research and conceptual background of the Q^{12} instrument is detailed in Harter and Schmidt (2000) and Harter, Schmidt, and Hayes (2002). In short, the Q^{12} was developed based on over thirty years of accumulated quantitative and qualitative research. Its reliability, convergent validity, and criterion-related validity have been extensively studied. It is an instrument validated through the above psychometric studies as well as practical considerations regarding its usefulness for managers in creating change in the workplace.

In designing the items included in the Q^{12}, researchers took into account that, from an actionability standpoint, there are two broad categories of employee survey items: those that measure attitudinal outcomes (satisfaction, loyalty, pride, customer service intent, and intent to stay with the company) and those that measure actionable issues that drive the above outcomes. In our standard set of Q^{12} items, we have included one outcome item (satisfaction with one's company) that can be seen as an overall measure of "satisfaction." Following the satisfaction item are twelve items measuring issues we have found to be actionable at the supervisor or manager level in the company—items measuring the extent to which employees are "engaged" in their work.

The twelve Q^{12} statements are as follows:

Q00. (Overall Satisfaction) On a five-point scale, where "5" is *extremely satisfied* and "1" is *extremely dissatisfied*, how satisfied are you with (name of company) as a place to work?

Q01. I know what is expected of me at work.

Q02. I have the materials and equipment I need to do my work right.

Q03. At work, I have the opportunity to do what I do best every day.

Q04. In the last seven days, I have received recognition or praise for doing good work.

Q05. My supervisor, or someone at work, seems to care about me as a person.

Q06. There is someone at work who encourages my development.

Q07. At work, my opinions seem to count.

Q08. The mission or purpose of my company makes me feel my job is important.

Q09. My associates or fellow employees are committed to doing quality work.

Q10. I have a best friend at work.

Q11. In the last six months, someone at work has talked to me about my progress.

Q12. This last year, I have had opportunities at work to learn and grow.

The current standard is to ask each employee to rate the above statements (a census survey—median participation rate is 79 percent), using six response options (from 5 = strongly agree to 1 = strongly disagree; the sixth response option—don't know/does not apply—is unscored). Because it is a satisfaction item, the first item is scored on a satisfaction scale rather than on an agreement scale.

As a total instrument (sum or mean of items 01–12), the Q^{12} has a Cronbach's alpha of 0.91 at the business-unit level. The meta-analytic convergent validity of the equally weighted mean (or sum) of items 01–12 (GrandMean) to the equally weighted mean (or sum) of additional items in longer surveys (measuring all known facets of job satisfaction and engagement) is 0.91. This provides evidence that the Q^{12}, as a composite measure, captures the general factor in longer employee surveys. Individual items correlate to their broader dimension true score values, on average, at 0.69.

As mentioned, Harter, Schmidt, and Hayes (2002) conducted an earlier version of this business unit–level meta-analysis. The current meta-analysis includes a larger number of studies, a larger number business units, more predictive data (that is, an increased number of the studies included in the present meta-analysis have business outcomes measured at some period after the Q^{12} measurement), and updated estimates of reliabilities and range restriction/variation across business units. This meta-analysis includes all available Gallup studies (whether published or unpublished) and has no risk of publication bias.

Meta-Analysis

A meta-analysis is a statistical integration of data accumulated across many different studies. As such, it provides uniquely powerful information, because it controls for measurement and sampling errors and other idiosyncrasies that distort the results of individual studies. A meta-analysis eliminates biases and provides an estimate of true validity or true relationship among two or more variables. Statistics typically calculated during meta-analyses also allow the researcher to explore the presence, or lack thereof, of moderators of relationships. More than one thousand meta-analyses have been conducted in the psychological, educational, behavioral, medical, and personnel selection fields. The research literature in the behavioral and social sciences includes a multitude of individual studies with apparently conflicting conclusions. Meta-analysis, however, allows the researcher to estimate the mean relationship between variables and make corrections for artifactual sources of variation in findings across studies. It provides a method by which researchers can determine whether validities and relationships generalize across various situations (for example, across firms or geographical locations).

This paper will not provide a full review of meta-analysis. Rather, the authors encourage readers to consult the following sources for both background information and detailed descriptions of the more recent meta-analytic methods: Schmidt (1992); Hunter and Schmidt (1990); Lipsey and Wilson (1993); Bangert-Drowns (1986); and Schmidt, Hunter, Pearlman, and Rothstein-Hirsh (1985).

Hypothesis and Study Characteristics

The hypotheses examined for this meta-analysis were as follows:

Hypothesis 1: Business unit–level employee satisfaction and engagement will have positive average correlations with the business unit outcomes of customer metrics, productivity, profitability, employee retention, and employee safety.

Hypothesis 2: The correlations between employee satisfaction and engagement and business unit outcomes will generalize across organizations for all business unit outcomes. That is, these correlations will not vary substantially across organizations, and in particular there will be few if any organizations with zero or negative correlations.

A total of sixty-eight studies for fifty-one independent companies are included in Gallup's inferential database—studies conducted as proprietary research for various organizations. In each Q^{12}, one or more of the Q^{12} items were used (as a part of standard policy, starting in 1997, all items were included in all studies), and data were aggregated at the business unit level and correlated with the following aggregate business unit performance measures:

- Customer metrics (referred to as customer loyalty)
- Profitability
- Productivity
- Turnover
- Safety

That is, in these analyses the unit of analysis was the business unit, not the individual employee.

Pearson correlations were calculated, estimating the relationship of business unit average measures of employee perceptions to each of these five general business outcomes. Correlations were calculated across business units within each company, and these correlation coefficients were entered into a database for each of the twelve items. The researchers then calculated mean validities, standard deviations of validities, and validity generalization statistics for each item for each of the five business unit outcome measures.

The overall study involved 308,987 independent employee responses to surveys and 10,885 independent business units in fifty-one companies, an average of 28 employees per business unit and 213 business units per company.

Table 1, which follows, provides a summary of studies (per company) sorted by industry type. It is evident that there is considerable variation in the industry types represented, as companies from twenty-three industries provided studies. Each of the five general government industry classifications (via SIC codes) is represented, with the largest number of companies represented in retail and services industries. The largest number of business units is in transportation and public utilities.

TABLE 1
Summary of Studies by Industry

Industry Type	Companies	Number of Business Units	Respondents
Financial—depository	5	1,927	26,389
Financial—security	4	255	5,182
Manufacturing—food	2	35	2,781
Manufacturing—instrument	1	8	164
Manufacturing—paper	1	60	17,243
Manufacturing—pharmaceutical	1	92	873
Manufacturing—printing	1	14	420
Retail—automotive	1	80	1,384
Retail—building materials	2	793	43,763
Retail—clothes	2	272	14,442
Retail—eating	5	367	21,103
Retail—entertainment	1	106	1,051
Retail—food stores	3	494	35,886
Retail—miscellaneous	3	949	47,491
Services—business	1	20	600
Services—education	3	200	1,747
Services—government	1	45	392
Services—health	5	791	35,314
Services—hotels	3	167	6,549
Services—recreation	1	14	288
Transport./public util.—trucking	1	96	6,213
Transport./public util.—comm.	2	4,039	35,964
Transport./public util.—electrical	2	61	3,748
Total Financial	9	2,182	31,571
Total Manufacturing	6	209	21,481
Total Retail	17	3,061	165,120
Total Services	14	1,237	44,890
Total Transportation/public util.	5	4,196	45,925
Total	51	10,885	308,987

Table 2 provides a summary of studies (per company) sorted by business unit type. There is also considerable variation in type of business unit, ranging from stores to plants/mills to departments. Overall, thirteen different types of business units are represented; most companies have business units consisting of stores, teams/departments, or bank branches. Teams/departments, stores, and bank branches had the highest proportional representation, in terms of number of business units.

TABLE 2
Summary of Business Unit Types

Business/Operating Unit Type	Companies	Number of Business Units	Respondents
Bank Branch	7	2,113	28,965
Call Center Department	2	52	2,024
City Center Office	3	64	2,612
Dealership	1	80	1,384
Healthcare Unit (hospital or office)	3	354	26,578
Hotel	1	36	3,124
Plant/Mill	2	72	19,805
Restaurant	5	367	21,103
Region	1	96	6,213
Sales Team	3	123	1,256
School	2	186	1,497
Store	11	2,614	142,633
Team/Department	10	4,728	51,793
Total	51	10,885	308,987

The following is the formula to calculate variance expected from sampling error in "bare bones" meta-analyses, using the Hunters and Schmidt (1990) technique:

$$S_e^2 = (1 - \bar{r}^2)^2 / (\bar{N} - 1)$$

Residual standard deviations were calculated by subtracting the amount of variance due to sampling error, the amount of variance due to study differences in measurement error in the dependent variable, and the amount of variance due to study differences in range variation from the observed variance. To estimate the true validity standard deviations, the residual standard deviation was adjusted for bias due to mean unreliability and mean range restriction. The amount of variance due to sampling error, measurement error, and range variation was divided by the observed variance to calculate the total percentage variance accounted for. One rule of thumb adopted from the literature is that, if over 75 percent of variance in validities across studies is due to sampling error and other artifacts, the validity is assumed generalizable.

Table 5 provides the correlation of overall satisfaction and engagement to composite performance. This calculation assumes managers are managing toward multiple outcomes simultaneously and that each outcome occupies some space in the overall evaluation of performance. To calculate the correlation to the composite index of performance, we used the Mosier (1943) formula to determine the reliability of the composite measure (as described in Harter et al., 2002), with updated reliability distributions and updated intercorrelations of the outcome measures. Because customer metrics, employee turnover, and financials are primary outcomes in most organizations, we again used these in our composite performance estimates. Composite performance was measured as the equally weighted sum of customer metrics, turnover (reverse scored as retention), and financials (with profitability and productivity equally weighted).

Results

Table 3 provides a summary of the items that had positive 90 percent credibility values (zero or negative for the turnover and safety measures) and in which over 75 percent of the variance in validities was accounted for. As can be seen, all items had relationships to all outcomes that were in the hypothesized direction, and nearly all of these relationships were generalizable. In fact, 90 percent of the effects studied in the item-level meta-analysis met these generalizability criteria. It is possible that those that did not were merely a function of second-order sampling error, since second-order sampling error analyses indicated high generalizability.

TABLE 3
Items with Meta-Analytic r's That Are
Generalizable Across Organizations

Item	Customer	Profitability	Productivity	Turnover	Safety
1) Know what is expected	x		x	x	x
2) Materials and equipment	x		x	x	x
3) Opp. to do what I do best	x	x	x	x	x
4) Recognition/praise	x	x	x	x	x
5) Cares about me	x	x	x	x	x
6) Encourages development	x	x	x	x	x
7) Opinions count	x	x	x	x	x
8) Mission/purpose	x		x	x	x
9) Committed—quality		x	x	x	x
10) Best friend	x	x	x		x
11) Talked about progress	x	x	x		x
12) Opps. to learn and grow	x	x	x	x	x

For purposes of overall evaluation of business units and for general theory building, it is useful to study composite measures of the satisfaction/engagement facets. That is, one general, global perception studied is "overall satisfaction with one's company" (defined by one item) and another is "overall employee engagement in one's work" (which is defined as the GrandMean of the Q^{12} items 01–12). Table 4 provides meta-analytic and validity generalization statistics for both of these "overall" indices, overall satisfaction (OS) and the GrandMean (GM) of items 01–12, the latter of which is a composite measure of employee engagement.

Since these "overall" indices lend themselves to general, theoretical inquiry, an additional correction was made to metaanalytic estimates—for range restriction in the independent variable across companies. Estimates that include this range-restriction correction apply to interpretations of effects in business units across companies, as opposed to effects expected within a given company. Because there is more variation in business units across companies than there is within the average company, effect sizes are higher when true validity estimates are calculated for business units across companies.

For instance, observe the estimates relative to the customer loyalty criteria. Without the between-company range restriction correction (which is relevant to the effect within the typical company), the true validity value of overall satisfaction is 0.21 with a 90 percent CV of 0.18. With the between-company range restriction correction (which is relevant to business units across companies), the true validity value of overall satisfaction is 0.30 with a 90 percent CV of 0.26. For employee engagement, all of the variance in correlations across studies is accounted for by sampling error. The true validity is the same as the 90 percent CV, which is 0.22 within a given company and 0.30 for business units across companies. Both OS and GM show generalizability across companies in their relationship to customer metrics, profitability, productivity, employee turnover, and safety outcomes. For profitability, GM demonstrated slightly more generalizability across companies. Effect sizes are of similar magnitude for the two "overall" measures.

In summary, for the overall measure of engagement shown in Table 4, the strongest effects were found relative to customer loyalty, employee turnover, productivity, and safety. Correlations were positive and generalizable relative to profitability criteria, but of lower magnitude. This may be because profitability is influenced indirectly by employee engagement and more directly by the customer, employee turnover, productivity, and safety. The next section will explore the practical utility of the observed relationships.

TABLE 4
Composite Incides (Overall Sat. and Q^{12} GrandMean)—Meta-Analysis

	Customer		Profitability		Productivity		Turnover		Safety	
	OS	GM	OS	GM	OS	GM	OS	GM	OS	GM
Number of Bus. Units	3339	3867	4381	4689	3816	4205	7611	8103	680	680
Number of r's	22	25	28	32	25	31	24	26	6	6
Mean Observed r	0.18	0.18	0.12	0.12	0.18	0.18	-0.15	-0.13	-0.17	-0.16
Observed SD	0.11	0.09	0.11	0.08	0.10	0.10	0.06	0.05	0.08	0.08
True Validity[1]	0.21	0.22	0.13	0.13	0.20	0.19	-0.21	-0.18	-0.22	-0.20
True Validity SD[1]	0.03	0.00	0.08	0.00	0.00	0.00	0.00	0.00	0.00	0.00
True Validity[2]	0.30	0.30	0.18	0.17	0.27	0.26	-0.29	-0.25	-0.29	-0.27
True Validity SD[2]	0.03	0.00	0.09	0.00	0.00	0.00	0.00	0.00	0.00	0.00
% Variance Acct'd For—										
Sampling error	55	83	51	93	67	72	82	116	123	144
%Variance Acct'd For[1]	95	135	69	114	116	107	196	215	177	186
%Variance Acct'd For[2]	98	138	69	115	118	108	203	219	180	187
90% CV[1]	0.18	0.22	0.05	0.13	0.20	0.19	-0.21	-0.18	-0.22	-0.20
90% CV[2]	0.26	0.30	0.07	0.17	0.27	0.26	-0.29	-0.25	-0.29	-0.27

OS = Overall Satisfaction
GM = GrandMean of Q^{12} items 01–12 (employee engagement)
SD = Standard Deviation

[1]Includes correction for range variation within companies and dependent-variable measurement error.
[2]Includes correction for range restriction across population of business units and dependent-variable measurement error.

As in Harter et al. (2002), we calculated the correlation of overall satisfaction and employee engagement with composite performance. As defined earlier, Table 5 provides the correlations and d-values for four analyses: the observed correlations, correction for dependent-variable measurement error, correction for dependent-variable measurement error and range restriction across companies, and correction for dependent-variable measurement error, range restriction, and independent-variable measurement error (true score correlation).

The effect sizes presented in Table 5 indicate very similar correlations of overall satisfaction and employee engagement with composite performance. Regression analyses (Harter et al., 2002) indicate that employee engagement accounts for nearly all of the performance-related variance (composite performance) accounted for by the overall satisfaction measure.

TABLE 5
Correlation of Employee Satisfaction and Engagement with Composite Business Unit Performance

Analysis	Satisfaction	Engagement
Observed r	0.23	0.23
d	0.37	0.37
r corrected for dependent-variable measurement error	0.27	0.27
d	0.44	0.44
r corrected for dependent-variable measurement error and range restriction	0.37	0.38
d	0.62	0.64
ρ corrected for dependent-variable measurement error, range restriction, and independent-variable measurement error	0.42	0.43
δ	0.71	0.73

Business units in the top half on engagement within companies have over 0.4 standard deviations units' higher composite performance in comparison to those in the bottom half on engagement. Across companies, business units in the top half on engagement have over 0.6 standard deviation units' higher composite performance in comparison to those in the bottom half on engagement.

Theoretically, after correcting for all available study artifacts, business units in the top half on employee engagement have over 0.7 standard deviation units' higher composite performance in comparison to those in the bottom half on engagement. This is the true score effect expected over time, across all business units.

Utility Analysis: Practicality of the Effects

In the past, studies of job satisfactions' relationship to performance have had limited analysis of the utility of the reported relationships. Correlations have often been discounted as trivial without an effort to understand the potential utility, in practice, of the relationships. The Q^{12} includes items Gallup researchers have found to be influenceable by the local manager. As such, understanding the practical utility of potential changes is critical.

The research literature includes a great deal of evidence that numerically small or moderate effects often translate into large practical effects (Abelson, 1985; Carver, 1975; Lipsey, 1990; Rosenthal and Rubin, 1982; Sechrest and Yeaton, 1982). Effect sizes referenced in this study are consistent with or above other practical effect sizes referenced in other reviews (Lipsey and Wilson, 1993).

Within companies, business units in the top half on employee engagement had, on average, a 56 percent higher success rate on customer loyalty (that is, [61% − 39%] /39% = 56.4%), a 44 percent higher success rate on turnover (lower probability of turnover), a 50 percent higher success rate on productivity outcomes, and a 33 percent higher success rate on profitability outcomes. For the additional safety variable (limited to six studies), business units in the top half on employee engagement had, on average, a 50 percent higher success rate (lower probability of lost workdays). For business units across companies, those in the top half on employee engagement had, on average, an 86 percent higher success rate on customer metrics, a 70 percent higher success rate on turnover (lower probability of turnover), a 70 percent higher success rate on productivity outcomes, a 44 percent higher success rate on profitability outcomes, and a 78 percent higher success rate on safety (lower probability of lost workdays).

Other forms of expressing the practical meaning behind the effects from this study include utility analysis methods (Schmidt and Rauschenberger, 1986). Formulas have been derived for estimating the dollar-value increases in output as a result of improved employee selection. These formulas can be used in estimating the difference in performance outcomes at different levels in the distribution of Q^{12} scores. Previous studies (Harter et al., 2002 and Harter and Schmidt, 2000) provided utility analysis examples, comparing differences in outcomes between the top and bottom quartiles on the twelve-item overall Q^{12} composite (GM). For companies included in this meta-analysis, it is typical to see differences between top and bottom engagement quartiles of 2–4 points on customer loyalty, 1–4 points on profitability, hundreds of thousands of dollars on productivity figures per month, and 4–10 points in turnover for low-turnover companies and 15–50 points for high-turnover companies. Such differences and their utility in dollar terms should be calculated for each company, given the company's unique metrics, situation, and distribution of outcomes across business units.

One can see that the above relationships are nontrivial if the business has many business units. The point of the utility analysis, consistent with literature that has taken a serious look at utility, is that the relationship between employee engagement and business outcomes, even conservatively expressed, is meaningful from a practical perspective.

Discussion

For an increased number of studies included in this updated meta-analysis, predictive data are included, with performance outcomes trailing the Q^{12} measurement. Across studies, correlations of Q^{12} items and overall indices to outcomes were widely generalizable, with variance in correlations attributable to sampling error and other artifacts. Consequently, the design of the study (predictive versus concurrent) was not considered as a moderator of the effect sizes. Evidence of directionality (through multiple time periods and path analysis) can be seen in individual case studies provided in *The Gallup Research Journal*. Path coefficients reported in such analyses are consistent with the magnitude that we have observed in this larger meta-analysis, which would suggest that, if moderators do exist, they may be limited.

Currently underway, and soon to be released, are meta-analyses of multiyear cross-lag correlations, examining the correlation of time 1 employee engagement to time 2 outcomes versus time 1 outcomes correlated with time 2 employee engagement. Of course, such analyses have been conducted for individual studies, but the meta-analyses currently in process will answer questions of directionality more precisely.

The most convincing causal evidence comes, not from one study, but from a body of research and a multitude of types of evidence, including qualitative analysis of high-performing business units, path analysis, predictive studies, and studies of change over time. Such individual studies are a part of Gallup's past and ongoing workplace management research practice.

It is also worth noting that, as Gallup consultants have educated managers and partnered with companies on change initiatives, companies have experienced (between the first and second year), on average, one half standard deviation growth on employee engagement, and often a full standard deviation growth and more after three or more years. A very important element in the utility of any applied instrument and improvement process is the extent to which the variable under study can be changed. Our current evidence is that employee engagement is to some extent changeable, and varies widely by business unit or workgroup.

In addition, work has been done showing that, at the individual level, employee satisfaction is at least somewhat trait related (Arvey, Bouchard, Segal, and Abraham, 1989; Bouchard, 1997). In the present analysis, for business units, we have averaged the independent variable across individuals, which makes our measure more a measure of business unit performance–related culture rather than of individual employee satisfaction. In averaging across individuals, we average out trait-related variations, producing a score that reflects the culture of the business unit.

Studies—both completed and in progress at Gallup—examining the relationship between changes in Q^{12} scores and changes in business outcomes add to the causal evidence of the relationship between business unit–level satisfaction/engagement and business unit results.

The authors conclude from this study, as with prior Gallup studies, that employee perceptions, as measured by Q^{12} items, relate to meaningful business outcomes, and that these relationships can be generalized across companies. The relationships observed are in the directions hypothesized and make psychological sense. Inferences of causality will depend on various pieces of evidence (outlined above) that are collected on an ongoing basis by Gallup researchers and client partner researchers. In addition, future research published in academic journals may help to shed additional light on the question of causality. Clearly, there are differences across business units in the way employees perceive their work environments, and these differences relate to differences in performance. The ongoing challenge in the days ahead is to continue to design programs that teach strategies for change. Such programs have been and remain a leading focus of The Gallup Organization.

Prepared by James K. Harter, Ph.D., and Frank L. Schmidt, Ph.D.

The authors thank Emily Killham, Jim Asplund, Sangeeta Badal, Donald O. Clifton, and the numerous Gallup researchers who contributed research studies, data sets, and their various forms of expertise to studies that have been included in this meta-analysis.

References

Abelson, R. P. (1985). A variance explanation paradox: When a little is a lot. *Psychological Bulletin, 97*, 129–133.

Arvey, R. D., Bouchard, T. J., Jr., Segal, N. L. & Abraham, L. M. (1989). Job satisfaction: Environmental and genetic components. *Journal of Applied Psychology, 74*, 187–192.

Bangert-Drowns, R. L. (1986). Review of developments in meta-analytic method. *Psychological Bulletin, 99* (3), 388–399.

Bouchard, T. J., Jr. (1997). Genetic influence on mental abilities, personality, vocational interests, and work attitudes. Chapter 9 in *Internal Review of Industrial and Organizational Psychology, 12*, 373–395. John Wiley & Sons Ltd.

Carver, R. P. (1975). The Coleman Report: Using inappropriately designed achievement tests. *American Educational Research Journal, 12*, 77–86.

Fleming, J. H. (Ed.). Linkage analysis (Special issue). (2000). *The Gallup Research Journal, 3* (1).

Harter, J. K. & Schmidt, F. L. (2000). *Validation of a Performance-Related and Actionable Management Tool:*

A Meta-Analysis and Utility Analysis. Princeton, NJ: The Gallup Organization.

Harter, J. K., Schmidt, F. L. & Hayes, T. L. (2002). Business unit–level relationship between employee satisfaction, employee engagement, and business outcomes: A meta-analysis. *Journal of Applied Psychology, 87, 2.*

Hunter, J. E. & Schmidt, F. L. (1990). *Methods of Meta-Analysis: Correcting Error and Bias in Research Findings.* Newbury Park, CA: Sage.

Lipsey, M. W. (1990). *Design Sensitivity: Statistical Power for Experimental Research.* Newbury Park, CA: Sage.

Lipsey, M. W. & Wilson, D. B. (1993). The efficacy of psychological, educational, and behavioral treatment. *American Psychologist, 48* (12), 1181–1209.

Mosier, C. I. (1943). On the reliability of a weighted composite. *Psychometrika, 8,* 161–168.

Rosenthal, R. & Rubin, D. B. (1982). A simple, general purpose display of magnitude of experimental effect. *Journal of Educational Psychology, 74,* 166–169.

Schmidt, F. L. (1992). What do data really mean? Research findings, meta-analysis, and cumulative knowledge in psychology. *American Psychologist, 47,* 1173–1181.

Schmidt, F. L., Hunter, J. E., Pearlman, K. & Rothstein-Hirsh, H. (1985). Forty questions about validity generalization and meta-analysis. *Personnel Psychology, 38,* 697–798.

Schmidt, F. L. & Rauschenberger, J. (1986, April). Utility analysis for practitioners. Paper presented at the First Annual Conference of The Society for Industrial and Organizational Psychology, Chicago.

Sechrest, L. & Yeaton, W. H. (1982). Magnitudes of experimental effects in social science research. *Evaluation Review, 6,* 579–600.

Acknowledgments

Our chairman and CEO, Jim Clifton, designed The Gallup Path. His theory has changed our understanding of the connections that govern the growth of organizations. The Gallup Path is the telescope that magnifies the scope of organizations throughout the world. In this way he is a twenty-first-century Galileo—someone who has defied the old, accepted view of his world and challenged us to see it in a new, more exciting, and more rewarding way.

We deeply appreciate his relentless pursuit to spark the fire inside each of his Gallup colleagues, his genuine and permanent passion for drawing out the best in each of us, and his creation of the emotional connections that propel us to grow to the highest of our potential in the search of significant discoveries.

Our gratitude also runs deep for Larry Emond and Geoff Brewer for their investment in our pearl diving, and their undying support to capture it and communicate it as loudly and clearly as possible. We deeply appreciate Ashok Gopal for his fruitful and intelligent input. We are also personally indebted to Susan Suffes, who helped us enhance the simplicity and clarity of our message.

We are indebted to our Gallup associates, particularly the guidance and support of Alec Gallup, Marcus Buckingham, Don Clifton, Guido de Koning, Eldin Ehrlich, John Fleming, Tom Hatton, Jim Harter, Jim Krieger, Deb Manning, Jan Miller, Bill McEwen, Denise McLain, Glenn Phelps, Adam

Pressman, Rosemary Travis, and Sarah Van Allen for their careful reviews and critical feedback, the fact checking of Mark Stiemann, and most of all the partnership of them all throughout this investigation. Thanks go to Rachel Penrod for keeping all of the pieces aligned and organized, Steve O'Brien and Evan Perkins for their guidance and counsel, and Jane Miller for her insightful "nuggets" along the way. And an appreciation goes to literally every Gallup associate, past and present. A piece of every one of you is in the spirit of this message.

Thanks also go to Joni Evans, our agent at William Morris, for her belief in us and her support, and to the folks at Warner Books and specifically our editor Rick Wolff for his enthusiastic support, trust, and superb advice.

There are so many friends whose support, love, and encouragement are literally found between the lines on every page. Thank you Becky, Steve, Nicholas and Alex, Adam, Amy, Ana-Maria, Benson, Bill, Bob and Amy, Bob and Carol Lee, Brad, Brenda, Brian, Cal, Carlo, Carlos, Chris and Bill, Connie, Connie, Craig and Anita, Dan, Deanna, Don and Betty, Ellen, Eric, Evan, Fran and Adriana, Frank, Frank, Gale, Gaylene, Geoff and Regan, Gonzalo, Greg, Govinsin, Hector and Gisela, Islet, Jack, Jacques and Diana, Dr. Jose Luis and Lupita, Julie, Jesus, Jim, Jim and Rae, John and Laura, John R., Julie, Karan, Kelly, Ken, Kevin, Larry and Julie, Selena, Larry and Howie, Laura, Leslie, Linda and Gregg, Linda, Mary and Mark, Max, Mike, Mom and Cliff, Nacho, Peter, Phil, Phil Paul, Randy, Holli, Corey and Sarah, Robby, Rafa, Rosa, Roy, Ruth, Sangeeta, Mons. Rosendo, Rachel and Rod, Robin, Rod, Jona and Luke, Ron, Scott, Sheila, Sonny, Steve, Steve, Steve, Todd, Tom, Tom, Tony, Troy and Misty, Yarisma and Mariana, and Warren.

And one more note of gratitude to probably our most important unending source of strength, our wives, Tammy and Belinda, along with our wonderful children Katie, Claire, Clayton, Gabriel, and Jose Ignacio.

ERICH

.70
250
0 0
350
.40
(75.00 =} 133 50 - 933
133. .
42.00 — C   YOUSAN   fromXO

                1) OFF 51 B   1

8.0
250   2) BUS STATION
40 0 0
.60   3)
200. 0 0

53
.250
26 50
.06